These sermons not only challenge our think[...] y
humble and inspire us to serve our pr[...]
the Gospel to ALL, no matter [...]
I thank the Lord for the work [...]
people crave a passion for the fo[...]
    Pastor Jonathan Pa[...]

[...] *ing For Life*

I first visited Nidrie Community Chur[...] 2014 and met many of the preachers in this book. Our church bought into their dream of planting churches in the poorest communities of Scotland, but, at the time, we never expected the abundant fruit of conversions, churches planted, leaders raised up, music produced, and books written. What do you say to a hopeless people who have not heard the gospel for generations? In short, it's not fluff. Not at all. 'The deepest wounds need the deepest doctrine.' Take up and read these sober, gritty, Christ-centred messages that give us a window into how to proclaim the gospel to those in desperate situations encouraging them to take up their cross and follow Jesus.

    Dr. Josh Vincent, Lead Pastor, Centreville Baptist Church, Northern Virginia

Kingdom work, whatever the environment, requires a love for Jesus and His Gospel and a love and understanding of the people with whom you are sharing the good news. We like to use big words, so we call it contextualisation. Those who are planting churches in the most socially deprived areas of Scotland understand that – in spades – and the wider church has much to learn from their commitment to the communities marginalised or forgotten by most. I commend this book for its wisdom, insight and practical grit.

    Derek Lamont, Senior pastor (22 years) St Columba's Free Church of Scotland, in the city centre of Edinburgh

Faithful contextualization is to remove all offense except the offense of the Gospel. Sermons From the Schemes is a model of how to faithfully proclaim God's word to people who are not used to feasting on it. This work will serve people who are far from God or those who have been walking with Him for decades.

    J. Garrett Kell, Pastor, Del Ray Baptist Church, Alexandria, Virginia

Full of wisdom and clear teaching, *Sermons from the Schemes* is a great resource. Pastors will benefit from this book's practical help for addressing difficult situations like poverty, addiction, and abuse. Preachers will benefit from this book's examples of how to communicate clearly without compromising content. Christians will benefit from this book's clear and Christ-exalting meditation on the way the gospel changes lives!

Mike McKinley, Senior Pastor, Sterling Park Baptist Church, Sterling, Virginia, USA

A useful collection of sermons from those who are preaching and teaching the Word of God faithfully in the Schemes of Scotland and Council Estates in England. Each sermon comes with the conviction that as the local church brings God's Word into the lives of broken people, God will be glorified, sinners saved and matured in Christ with the hope of eternal life.

This book will do your heart good being reminded of the great love of God and it will help keep your hand on the plough as you persevere in ministry.

Stuart Davis, Pastor, Trinity Road Chapel, Wandsworth, London

From the trenches of the schemes comes a treasure-trove of biblical truth and encouragement. This little book is big on the Gospel, the church, and God's people. 20schemes pastors and Gospel workers present the Gospel, the nature, and work of a healthy church. It's a reminder that preaching to the poor should not be simplistic. Those neglected by society should not be neglected in the best of our teaching and preaching. This book is not only model, but comfort for the weary and encouragement for the faithful.

Joel Kurz, Pastor at The Garden Church, Baltimore, Maryland, USA, and Director of ONE HOPE

20schemes

SERMONS FROM THE SCHEMES

Teaching and preaching the Bible among Scotland's poorest

Edited by Mez McConnell

Grace Publications

Grace Publications Trust
62 Bride Street
London N7 8AZ
www.gracepublications.co.uk

First Published in Great Britain by Grace Publications Trust in 2023

The right of 20schemes to be identified as the author of this work has been asserted by them under the Copyright, Designs and Patents act 1988.

©20schemes, 2023

No part of this publication may be reproduced, stored in a retrieval system or transmitted in any form by any means, electronic, mechanical, photocopying, recording or otherwise, without the prior permission of the publisher or the Copyright Licensing Agency.

A record for this book is available from the British Library.

Scripture quotations in Chapters 1, 2, 6, 8, 10, 11, 12 and 14 are taken from the New International Version (NIV). Holy Bible, New International Version®, NIV® Copyright ©1973, 1978, 1984, 2011 by Biblica, Inc.® Used by permission. All rights reserved worldwide.

Scripture quotations in Chapters 3, 4, 5, 9 and the Epilogue are taken from the English Standard Version (ESV). The Holy Bible, English Standard Version. ESV® Text Edition: 2016. Copyright © 2001 by Crossway Bibles, a publishing ministry of Good News Publishers.

Scripture quotations in Chapter 7 are taken from the Christian Standard Bible. Copyright © 2017 by Holman Bible Publishers. Used by permission. Christian Standard Bible®, and CSB® are federally registered trademarks of Holman Bible Publishers, all rights reserved.

Scripture quotations in Chapter 13 are taken from the New American Standard Bible®, Copyright © 1960, 1971, 1977, 1995, 2020 by The Lockman Foundation. All rights reserved.

Cover design by Pete Barnsley (CreativeHoot.com)

ISBN Paperback: 978-1-912154-83-8
Ebook: 978-1-912154-84-5

Printed and bound in Great Britain by Ashford Colour Press

Contents

Acknowledgements 7

Foreword 9
    Matthew Spandler-Davison

Introduction 11
    Mez McConnell

1. The message of the church:
What is the gospel? 13
    Andy Prime

2. Evangelism 31
    Ian Williamson

3. The cost of discipleship 47
    Matthew Spandler-Davison

4. Worship in the schemes:
Learning to lament 61
    Sol Fenne

5. Prayer 73
    Chris Davidson

6. The church:
What is it and why is it so important? 91
    Andy Constable

7. Membership:
How church membership killed our church plant and why I'm glad it did 105
    Pete Stewart

8. Doctrine:
Atonement and election – the gift of salvation applied to the graft of Ministry 117
    Andy Prime

9. Dealing with discipline 135
    Mez McConnell

10. Preaching to the working class 151
    Ian Williamson

11. Abuse and the gospel 163
    Mez McConnell

12. Addictions 175
    Mez McConnell

13. Women's ministry and the Word:
Trust God's word as sufficient for all circumstances and situations 189
    Sharon Dickens

14. Diversity 203
    Andy Constable

Epilogue:
Perseverance when we hit the wall 219
    Andy Constable

Acknowledgements

Thanks must go to each of the contributors for their time and efforts. Of course, all praise and honour goes to Christ. Without him, we would have no hope to hold out. Without the Bible we would have no message to teach.

Sermons From The Schemes

Foreword

Matthew Spandler-Davison
Acts29 VP Global Outreach and 20schemes Executive Director

In 2012, 20schemes began with a vision to see healthy churches started or revitalised in the schemes of Scotland. Since then, by God's grace, churches are gathering in deprived communities in Edinburgh, Glasgow, Dundee and Inverness. Most people attending these churches have no history of going to church and have probably never listened to a sermon before. As people come to know the Lord and are discipled in the local church we have to be able to preach, teach and counsel in such a way that makes sense to those who live in our working class communities. Mez McConnell excels at doing just that. His own life story is one of growing up in deep poverty and battling with abuse and addictions. He did not have a upbringing in the church and came to faith after serving time in prison. The language of the street is his mother tongue and the effectiveness of his ministries in England, Brazil, and Scotland over the last 30 years are testimony to that. Mez has the rare ability to communicate deep truths in simple and meaningful ways without dumbing them down. That can also be said for those who have been trained to lead the 20schemes church plants.

This book is a collection of sermons or talks that have been given by 20schemes church planters and ministry leaders over the last 10 years. They speak to real issues that real people in working class communities struggle with. They serve as examples for how to communicate effectively in deprived communities. However, this collection of sermons provides more than just a model for how to give a sermon; they are in themselves instructive and helpful for those seeking to engage areas of deprivation. As you read them you will find help to disciple, counsel, evangelise and pray with people living in schemes, council estates and other poor communities.

I trust that this book will be both an encouragement and a help to you as you seek to minister to those living in poverty near you.

Introduction
Mez McConnell

When Matthew Spandler-Davison and I started 20schemes in 2012, our vision was to plant, or revitalise, 20 gospel-loving churches in 20 of Scotland's poorest housing schemes.

At that time there was no serious discussion or interest in the broader UK church about planting in these communities. Lots of good para-church work was going on but none of it was really joined up, and very little of it was growing and establishing local Christians in local churches.

As the ministry began to grow, we made the decision to start two weekend conferences a year. There were maybe 20 to 30 of us at our first weekend event where we worshipped God and studied the Bible together. Our concern was to preach the Word to the concerns of those living and working in housing schemes. We were very clear from the outset that we wanted people to come to our 'weekenders' and leave feeling encouraged, but underwhelmed. We wanted people to leave with the feeling, 'We could do that.'

I deliberately kept the numbers to under 100 people, so that we could keep the family feel of the events. I only invited preachers who were working in our context, and we shared testimonies of new believers from around Scotland. Keeping it small ensured that we had time to answer questions and to socialise with one another. Weekenders still remain my favourite part of the year.

A couple of years in, we began a pre-weekender event for women, led by Sharon Dickens. The intention here was to encourage women working and living in poor communities. This is why we have included one of Sharon's messages in the book. (We kept the title, *Sermons From The Schemes*, even though technically it should be called, *Sermons From The Schemes, apart from Sharon's chapter which was taught by her to a group of women.* I am not sure the publisher would have appreciated that!)

What we have done is collate 14 messages out of a pool of many more, which seek to apply the word of God to some of the more complicated issues we face in ministry to housing schemes.

I hope they encourage your soul to the glory of Jesus.

1. The message of the church: What is the gospel?

Andy Prime
Gracemount Community Church, Edinburgh

Imagine arriving at the scene of a multi-car accident, with smoke billowing, cars upturned and mangled, debris strewn across the road, multiple people injured or dead, screams piercing the air and sirens blaring. What do we do? How do we prioritise who we should help first? This is where triage comes in.

Triage is assessing *need* and prioritising the *neediest*. Triage means that we attend to the young child with a huge gash in their forehead before we deal with the man who has injured his arm. Or, even if we're dealing with one person, we would apply pressure to a bleeding wound before we give our attention to their broken finger.

Let's change the image slightly. We arrive at the scene of the Titanic moments after it struck the iceberg. We're met with a harrowing image of hundreds of people floating in the water

– some alive, others dead. How do assess priority of care? Who requires our immediate attention and who can wait? This is how triage works.

Let's think a bit more deeply about those hundreds of souls in the water. Let's think about some of their personal problems. Some of them are probably unemployed. It would be safe to assume that some of them would be battling one mental illness or another. Maybe a few of them have cancer. Some of them may be divorced, others having illicit affairs. Some of them may be very nice people, and others terrible human beings. Yet, none of these things would matter at that moment in that cold, deadly water.

We wouldn't care about those things as we rushed to people's aid. We wouldn't begin a marriage counselling session with a warring couple trying to stay afloat on a piece of debris. That would be ridiculous. They have more pressing issues than their marital problems. They need to get out of that water before they die of exposure.

In the same way, we wouldn't pull a drunk passenger onto our lifeboat and then begin an AA meeting with him or her. The pressing issue isn't saving them from their alcoholism, it's saving their life.

We wouldn't start by handing out food parcels to people floating in the icy water. They may well need a hot meal, but their bigger need is to get out of the water and into a safe place.

As Christians we live and work in communities with thousands of people. Between them, they will have hundreds of thousands of personal issues. Some will be more serious than others. How do we begin to help them? How do we prioritise the greatest need? How do we do 'spiritual triage' in the chaos of our broken communities?

The spiritual priority of the gospel

Before we do anything, we must ask ourselves a question, and it's this: 'What is the gospel?' The number one rule of spiritual triage is that the greatest need of every soul in our care, whether they recognise it or not, is an appreciation of, and a trust in, the gospel of Jesus Christ. We're fully aware that our churches are full of people with pastoral issues to deal with and there are many ministries requiring our attention. People will be in various states of distress, some more pressing and chaotic than others. But the greatest need of every soul in our care is trust in the gospel of Jesus Christ.

Maybe our family situation feels like a battleground. There are tensions in our marriage. Maybe we have a toddler with behavioural issues. Maybe we have a stroppy teen. Maybe we have fallen out with some of our wider family members. Maybe we feel hopeless and helpless in the middle of it all. Regardless, our primary ministry is to live, witness to, and proclaim the gospel in the middle of all this carnage.

Maybe we feel like our church is too small and underequipped to meet the huge and diverse needs of our scheme, or our town, or our village, or our city, or our nation. Still, it doesn't matter whether it is a professor from the academy, or an MP from parliament, or a homeless person under a bridge, or a child in the most privileged school in the country, or an orphan in the hamster-wheel of the fostering system, or a single-mum addicted to Valium. We all have the same greatest and most urgent need.

We need to hear the gospel of the Lord Jesus Christ.

If we take time to do a biblically-informed spiritual triage of our communities, the greatest need is not social reform, or more foodbanks, or more homeless shelters, or improved education, or fresh expressions of church, or whatever. Doubtless, some of these things are required, but the situation requires a much deeper solution.

The need is for Christians, who in being discipled to apply the gospel to themselves, are equipped to apply the gospel to the world.

The danger of a wrong gospel

A lot of well-meaning Christians think that helping the needy requires some other approach. But the urgent priority is ensuring that we have a crystal-clear understanding of the gospel, and on how it applies to *all of us*. Some of us may talk a lot about 'the gospel,' yet what we articulate is *not*, in fact, the *true gospel*.

Maybe we go for something like, 'God loves you and wants you to live a better life.' Or 'God loves you and has a wonderful plan for your life.' Or 'God's kingdom has come in Jesus, and now he calls us to work with him to transform every aspect of society.' These soundbites may well contain some nuggets of truth, but they are *not* the *true gospel*.

The message of the church

A false or even an incomplete gospel is like a placebo. It might fool the patient into thinking they will get better, but it doesn't have the power to cure them. There can be no gospel ministry and, ultimately, no hope for sin-sick sufferers if we don't get the gospel right.

Others of us, however, can preach and explain the intricate doctrines of the Christian faith, yet we have no idea about what to do with the practical realities of ministry to needy people. Indeed, we often struggle to apply the gospel to ourselves!

I've known professors of biblical theology whose lives were consumed by bitterness and rage towards fellow Christians. I've known pastors who will preach week by week, and whose private lives are enslaved to porn. I've known elders, tasked to keep watch over the household of God, whose home lives have been characterised by abuse and wild, exasperated children. I've known youth leaders who teach the Scriptures to children the morning after a drinking binge and a night in bed with a non-Christian boyfriend.

True theology must always be applied. Dead orthodoxy isn't theology. I was once told, 'You have never truly understood something until you can explain it simply.' Let me adjust that slightly, 'We have never truly believed something, until we have obeyed and applied it.' Any true knowledge of God will result in application – praise, worship, confession, etc.

There can be no gospel ministry and, ultimately, no hope for sin-sick sufferers if we don't believe and apply the gospel to ourselves. We cannot offer what we do not possess. We cannot offer a life-transforming gospel if that gospel hasn't transformed our own life. The gospel is never simply something *explained*, it is *experienced*. It is never simply something *accomplished*, it is something *applied*.

So, what then, is the gospel?

The message is infinitely deep and wide, but we can summarise it under four headings: God, Man, Christ, and Response.

God

The gospel begins and ends with God. It begins with his unchanging character and sovereign choices in eternity. It ends with saved sinners enjoying him forever. If God hadn't chosen to save sinners, we would still be dead in sin, rather than enjoying his salvation.

God is the infinite, eternal, holy creator of all things. He alone is worthy of all praise, honour, and glory. As the *Holy, Holy, Holy God*, his eyes are too pure to look upon evil (Hab. 1:13), and so he will not leave sin unpunished (Ex. 34:7).

Our experience in the schemes of Scotland is that there is an innate supernaturalistic worldview among most people. They have no problem believing that some form of supernatural entity or 'god' exists. You won't find many intellectually convinced atheists on a housing scheme.

Take Maddie for example. Maddie's partner died from an overdose. He was sometimes abusive and often absent, but – as the father of her three children – she loved him deeply. Every year, on the anniversary of his death, she grieves. One day, she announces that she was going to the local spiritualist church – a church, by the way, where you have to pay at the door to enter. Why? Because there's a long-ingrained concept of life-beyond-death, and there's a deep hurt that yearns for an answer; coupled with a desire to keep living the party-girl lifestyle.

Or take Coleen. A single mum, battling addiction and trying to keep a sense of control through her chronic eating disorder. One day she mentions that she regularly goes to see a psychic. Why? Because, rolling with the punches as she flies from crisis to crisis, struggling with the mundane and lonely nature of her day-to-day, she *longs* for good news. And if she can't see it in her present reality, she looks for it in a future fantasy.

The issue is not that people *don't* believe in God. The problem lies with *the kind of god that they believe in*. They view God as irrelevant; disinterested; and lenient.

Therefore, it is essential that we proclaim the character of God among the poor. We must present a God who is holy and who will hold them accountable. This is a direct attack on their amoral approach to life. We must present a God who can be known and who, in Christ, has revealed himself perfectly to sinful people. Essentially, this is what Maddie and Coleen and all the thousands who live in the schemes need to know:

- God is God – and you are not
- You are created by him – and so you are accountable to him
- God is not naturally knowable – but he has made himself known
- You are designed by him – and so you are defined by him

- You are purposed by him – and so your purpose is to live for him.

Anything else you live for is not only dead, nothing, worthless and ignorant, but it is disobedient, rebellious, self-loving and idolatrous. This is what Maddie and Coleen need to hear.

Maddie, the answer to the reality of death will *not* be found in the spiritualist church. The answer to the pain of death will be found in the Author of Life. But the answer is not one that you can pick and choose depending on your fancy, or to fit around your lifestyle. It comes from the Sovereign King who won't pander to your imagination, but before whom you must bow the knee.

Coleen, proper, true good news in the face of the tough everyday will not come from the meanderings of a psychic's mind. It will come first as you acknowledge that you are accountable for the poor decisions you have made in the past and acknowledge that God is the source of all good decisions in the future. God is good, and he has demonstrated that in so many concrete ways.

Us

Created in the image of God, all humanity has a humble dignity – we are created to relate to God, to rule under him and to find our rest in him. However, Genesis 1–3 and Romans 1 teach us that:

- Instead of *relating to him*, we want to be him. We are created in God's image to be like him – but, instead, we want the knowledge of good and evil for ourselves, in order to be God
- Instead of *ruling under* him, we want to rule *instead* of him
- Instead of *finding rest in him*, we rebelliously try and find rest in his creation with no reference to him.

As a result, we run a relentless, restless race towards hell. According to Ephesians 2, we're dead in our sin, following the prince of the power of the air, living in disobedience, satisfying the passions of our flesh, and living according to our nature as children of wrath.

Most of us have a sliding scale when it comes to sin. As long as we feel that we are not harming people or not at the bad end of the spectrum, then we feel sure we are going to be alright.

I once visited a man in prison who's there because of a lifetime of alcohol- and drug-fuelled abuse of his wife and children, culminating in him being arrested drunk in charge of a car for which he had no licence or insurance. Searched by police at the scene, they discovered a knife and a series of texts on his phone threatening to stab his wife. I sat in that prison visiting hall and listened as he self-righteously acquitted himself and condemned the others in the prison as 'monsters' who were there for 'serious' crimes.

There is always something in all of us that will find someone else who's worse than we are, in order to make ourselves feel better.

We all make excuses – and none more so than those who live in our schemes. Victim mentality runs deep in our communities. 'It's not my fault' could be the motto for a lot of the people in the schemes. Add to that the fact that most counselling from therapists and social workers fills our heads with the idea that we are good people who have been put in bad circumstances, and it all adds up to us being victims. There's nothing to say sorry for, but plenty to grumble about. Inside of all of us is the crafty weasel that instinctively offloads blame on to anyone but ourselves – even God.

The Bible confronts this entitled, victim mentality. James writes, 'each person is tempted when they are dragged away by their own evil desire and enticed. Then, after desire has conceived, it gives birth to sin; and sin, when it is full-grown, gives birth to death' (Jas. 1:14–15).

Here's the point: my sin, and my death, come from *my evil desires*. I sin because *I want to sin*. I sin because *I choose to sin*. I sin because *I desire to sin*.

The Bible teaches us that *desires* give birth to sin, and sin gives birth to *death*. Death is not just something that happens to us, it is something that is *deserved by us*. My death will be a result of *my evil desires*. James is clear: your death is a result of your sin, and your sin is a result of your desires. Every person in hell will be able to trace back how they got there to *their own evil desires*. That's what Paul means in Romans 1 when he tells us that we are, 'without excuse' (Rom. 1:20).

Of course, we are all victims of sin to one degree or another – whether it's abuse at the hands of another, or neglect and an absence of love. There is a place for compassion and mercy and sympathy. But the Bible never allows us to use the actions of others as an excuse for our own sins.

Those of us seeking to help people in needy areas must encourage them to see themselves, not primarily as victims, but as sinners and wilful rebels. Putting our arm around their shoulder and just telling them that Jesus loves them, and that it is going to be all right, is not doing them any favours.

The most loving thing we can do for people in the schemes is *not* to help them with their electricity bill, or to help them find work, or to clean them up, or to give them a bed, or help with their drug habit. The most loving thing we can do for our fellow human beings is to proclaim to them the reality and seriousness of hell.

Unless we help those who are poor to see themselves as the Bible does, we ultimately leave them trapped and helpless like a hamster in a wheel. They will be destined to see themselves at the centre of a world that is all about them and their problems. But when we help the poor to understand themselves as God sees them, then we open up the door to real, deep, gospel transformation.

Getting this right is crucial, because if we misdiagnose the problem, then we will prescribe the incorrect solution.

Christ

The answer to sin, our problem, is Jesus Christ. In Mark 5, we meet three people: Legion the demon possessed man, Jairus whose daughter dies, and an unnamed bleeding woman. What unites them all is their *utter hopelessness*. They, or the people around them, are resigned to the inevitability and inescapability of their problems.

Of Legion, we read that 'no one could bind him anymore' and 'no one was strong enough to subdue him' (verses 3 and 4). The woman 'had suffered a great deal under the care of many doctors and had spent all she had, yet instead of getting better she grew worse' (verse 26). And Jairus is told that, 'Your daughter is dead ... Why bother the teacher anymore?' (verse 35). No-one's strong enough. Nothing's worked. Don't bother.

It's tempting to develop that same mind-set and worldview when dealing with people from the schemes. The problems are so deep-rooted; the cycles have been unbroken for generations; the scenarios are so complicated.

However, the three individuals in Mark 5 are not only united by their despair. See their responses on meeting Jesus: in verse 6, 'When [Legion] saw Jesus from a distance, he ran and fell on his knees in front of him'; in verse 22, 'When [Jairus] saw Jesus, he fell at his feet'; in verse 33, 'Then the woman, knowing what had happened to her, came and fell at his feet'.

When we're at the end of ourselves, and we've exhausted every other option, all that is left is to fall at the feet of Jesus. That's why we need to be careful of using language such as, '*no-one's strong enough*' or '*why bother*' when Jesus is in the room. It doesn't matter if we're mentally unhinged and living naked in a cave, or a powerful leader brought to our knees in bereavement, or a woman who's exhausted all medical help, all *can* and *must* fall on their face at the feet of Jesus.

The answer to our sin problem is Jesus Christ. In his life, Jesus Christ modelled the perfect standard of holiness and righteousness that God requires. In his miracles, Jesus Christ gives glimpses and demonstrations of what his future kingdom is going to be like. On the cross, Jesus Christ died as a substitute in our place – bearing our sin, our guilt, our shame, our curse. When he rose, Jesus Christ swallowed the oppressive reign of death, obliterating the enslaving reign of sin, as the first fruits and foretaste of the eternal reign of grace.

We don't find that anywhere else. Many in our scheme are like the woman in Mark 5: they've tried everything – legal and illegal, doctors and dealers, mediums and faith healers, spending all they have. But, instead of getting better, they get worse. The point is, we don't find this anywhere else. It is found only in Christ.

If that is true, people *must* believe the true gospel in order to be saved and brought into a right relationship with God. There is salvation in *no one else*. There is no back-up plan. People in our housing schemes will only be saved if they hear the gospel word proclaimed to them in a clear and comprehensible manner. There is no other way.

This is the Jesus that the poor need: a sin-bearing, atonement-making, guilt-cleansing, living Redeemer. A Christ who will call us what we are – sinners. But a Christ who will then speak with sinners, associate with sinners, eat with sinners, and then *die for sinners*.

Response

When we are confronted with the reality of our problem before a holy God, our instinctive response is often wrong. That applies both to unbelievers from a completely un-churched background, as well as well-meaning Christians trying to help.

Steven is one of my neighbours, born and raised in the scheme. He has the exterior of a pit-bull and a temper of a loose cannon. Yet, deep down, he is as soft as a teddy bear. He's recently started reading the Bible with me, and given his run-ins with the police, constant fighting with neighbours over parking and volatile relationship with his partner, he is very conscious of his sin. In his mind there is *no doubt* that he has fallen short of God's standard.

However, because of an ingrained and instinctive cultural Catholicism, the solution for him is to visit a local priest for confession. It's a quick-fix, easy, costless remedy. We managed to talk him out of that and encouraged him to come to one of our Sunday services. So far so good. However, we need to be careful that in our excitement at his appearance, we don't miss the fact that we could merely be compounding an incorrect response to his own sin. Mere church attendance is not an adequate response to his sin any more than confessing to a priest is.

Nicola is a girl on the scheme. She's got restraining orders on just about everybody, and she could start a fight with her own reflection! She's floated in and out of the local Church of Scotland congregation for a few years. She recently got pregnant because of a brief relationship with a drug-user who wants nothing to do with her or the baby. Outwardly she's happy; inwardly she's petrified and isolated.

When she announced this to a woman from the Church of Scotland, the response she got was, 'You know you should really get married to the father of the baby.' The problem is, although Nicola's floating in and out of church, she's not claiming to be a Christian. Therefore, by imposing Christian behaviour on her, she is being asked to produce the fruit of the Spirit before she's even responded to the gospel. It's unreasonable to expect Christian behaviour from someone who's not a Christian. We are asking them to do something they are completely incapable of. It is setting them up for failure. It is feeding them food we know will make them sick. This sort of moral advice is not going to help her.

The biblical response to her problem is repentance from sin, and faith in Christ.

Biblical repentance looks like this:

(1) It begins in *a heart transformed by the gospel*. They don't just see their sin, they own it, and soon, they hate it.
(2) This is then *verbalised* in a confession of faith in the gospel, repenting of sin and believing the promises of God.
(3) This then results in a *transformed life* that bears the fruit of repentance.

We do not help them if we merely teach them part (2). We must earnestly pray for (1), as well as present the necessity and certain cost of (3).

Conclusion

People from broken, chaotic and messy lives are all different and, therefore, repentance does not always look the same for everyone. Mental issues and sexual abuse complicate things further. For people in messy situations, repentance is going to involve making hard decisions and dealing with the consequences of a selfish and sinful lifestyle.

How about the man who has three children by two different women, who wants to turn from his sinful, abusive past, come to Christ and be a proper father to his children? What does repentance look like for him? It's not going to be simple and clean. In his book, *Church in Hard Places*, Mez McConnell tells the following story:

> Take Innocencia, a 13-year-old street girl from northern Brazil. She had lived on the streets for most of her short life. Her parents abandoned her at 5 years old and from the age of 6 onwards she had sold her body for sex to pay for food and to feed her glue habit. When we found her, she was in a mess. One of her arms had been crippled from a beating she took on the streets from a punter, all her teeth were missing, and she had been raped countless times. One day, when she heard the life transforming truth about God, her sinful position before him, and the good news of what Jesus had done, she wanted to repent on the spot. We prayed with her and trusted that she had made a genuine profession of faith. Several days later we found Innocencia barely conscious in the streets, a bag of industrial strength glue at her feet … My Brazilian team were devastated and angry; her repentance had seemed so

genuine! We got her to her feet, cleaned her up at our centre, and spoke to her about the commitment she had made to Christ. 'Oh, Pastor Mez,' she said, 'I do love Jesus. I have turned from my sin. Last night I turned a client down and I am now only doing 6 bags a day instead of 10.' She beamed at me with pride, and I felt chastened. Was I really expecting that she'd be a finished product on day 1 of conversion?[1]

Response is more than just a confession of Christ, but because it involves a *lifetime* of repentance, our strategy must involve a *lifetime* of discipleship. We are called not to get conversions, but to make obedient disciples. The response required from them is the whole of themselves, for the rest of their life. Therefore, the ministry needed by us must be to give the whole of our lives, to model discipleship that perseveres until the very end.

---

1   Mez McConnell, *Church in Hard Places,* Crossway, 2016.

2. Evangelism

Ian Williamson
Executive Director of Medhurst Ministries[1]

Funerals are perhaps one of the most difficult things to attend unless you're the one being buried! Many of my friends and family find them too hard to bear and so they often don't turn up, unless completely necessary, such as for a close family member or friend. Even though I personally struggle with funerals, I go as a sign of my love and/or respect for the person who has died. Sometimes friends will say: *'Funerals aren't my thing. I'm not the type of person who goes to funerals.'* I want to ask, 'What type of people go to funerals?' It seems such a strange thing to say.

What I find more surprising is that many Christians say almost the same thing about evangelism. Often, people will confide to me that they're just not built to be evangelists. It isn't their thing. It's not their gift. 'It's OK *for you,*' they say. *'Evangelism comes naturally to you. You're such an extrovert and*

---

[1] Otherwise known as the fat lad who cries!

so it's easier for you than it is for me.' Again, to me, this sounds like such a strange thing to say.

For the record I am *not* a natural evangelist, nor an extrovert. The reason I evangelise is the same reason I go to the funeral of family members and friends. I do it because it's expected of me, and it shows my love for Jesus who died for my sins, rose again, ascended to heaven, and will one day return for his church and to judge the living and the dead.

The weight of evangelism

Consider the words in Luke 12:48, 'From everyone who has been given much, much will be demanded; and from the one who has been entrusted with much, much more will be asked.' We have been given no greater gift than the gospel, and we have no greater stewardship than to share that message of good news with others. Paul expresses it well in 2 Corinthians 5:14. 'For Christ's love compels us.' That is a heavy weight to bear for *every* Christian, regardless of personality type.

I believe that part of the failure of individual Christians to step up to evangelism lies with the current culture of churches relying on courses to do a job they themselves should be doing personally and naturally. Why are there so many courses equipping Christians for evangelism, and yet so few people out doing the work on the ground? It's not that these courses are bad tools. They can be extremely helpful. But when we reduce evangelism to a crash course that must be done in a certain way and taught by trained theologians, it can weaken the church, instead of strengthening it.

It's not that some of these courses and training materials are not helpful, they clearly are. It's just that if we are not careful, they can inadvertently reduce evangelism to something only done by the specially trained or by those who are a bit more extrovert than others. All Christians, regardless of educational background and culture are duty bound to spread the good news of Jesus. And all Christians filled with the Holy Spirit of God, with a love for Jesus and the Word, have everything they need to evangelise the lost.

The priority of evangelism

We read the following in Colossians 1:28-29, 'He is the one we proclaim, admonishing and teaching everyone with all wisdom, so that we may present everyone fully mature in Christ. To this end I strenuously contend with all the energy Christ so powerfully works in me.'

And Mark 2:1-2, 'A few days later, when Jesus again entered Capernaum, the people heard that he had come home. They gathered in such large numbers that there was no room left, not even outside the door, and he preached the word to them.'

In Mark 1 we discover that Jesus had healed many people of illness, driven away many demons and even healed a leprous man. Naturally, a crowd gathered when they heard that Jesus was in town! There would have been all sorts of people with all sorts of needs in that crowd. Some wanted physical healing, others possibly spiritual healing, others just to be entertained by miracles, and still others who wanted nothing more than to discredit him.

The house Jesus was in was full, and the streets outside were full. It was an intense gathering of desperate and excited people, each one straining to get a look at Jesus. Doubtless, there was a lot of angry pushing and shoving as people tried to get as near to the action as they could.

Yet despite the chaos, and despite the many different reasons why the crowd had come to see him, despite the seriousness of their needs, Jesus uses this opportunity of a fixed audience to preach the Word to them all. It is clear that preaching the gospel is Jesus' main priority.

The churches in our communities are constantly dealing with a seemingly never-ending queue of desperate people struggling with addiction, mental health, bereavement and other life-consuming problems. People come to us for any number of reasons. Maybe they heard about how our church helped a friend or family members of theirs. Maybe some of them are curious about what goes on in our churches. Many of them are certainly desperate for help of one kind or another.

What we need to remember in our dealings with suffering people is that our priority must be preaching the gospel to them.

We are not saying that we won't help people if we can. We are making it known to them that what *they* think their primary need is differs from what *we* as Christians know it to be. They need to hear the gospel and we need to be always prepared to share it with them.

Evangelism becomes so much easier when our churches have the same reputation as Jesus. Are we known for our compassion and practical help and care for the suffering? Great. We should be. Are we also known for preaching the gospel to every soul we encounter, regardless of need? Remember that nothing shows our compassion and care for the lost quite like the unashamed preaching of the gospel.

Overcoming obstacles in our evangelism

We read this in Mark 2:3–5:

> Some men came, bringing to him a paralyzed man, carried by four of them. Since they could not get him to Jesus because of the crowd, they made an opening in the roof above Jesus by digging through it and then lowered the mat the man was lying on. When Jesus saw their faith, he said to the paralyzed man, 'Son, your sins are forgiven.'

After hearing of Jesus ability to heal, a group of men decide to take their disabled friend to see Jesus. But, when they get to the place he is at, they can't get near because of the crowds. In desperation, they smash through the roof of the house and lower their paralysed friend down through the hole they had made. These are good friends! These are men not easily put off by the obstacles they faced in getting their friend to Jesus. They didn't give up when it seemed impossible. They had faith and they took risks.

Sometimes I get put off introducing people to Jesus because I get scared. Sometimes, it's because I think the obstacles in the way are so big. I look at people's lifestyles, their religious beliefs, their addictions, their sexuality, and I think that they are too far gone to be saved. Therefore, I reason, *Why even bother evangelising them?* Far too often I give up at the first obstacle, when I should be like the friends of the paralysed man who are so desperate to introduce their mate to Jesus that they smash their way through every obstacle that gets in their way. When it comes to evangelism, we will always come up against obstacles, not least our own lack of zeal.

We must prayerfully persist in our evangelism, even if many of our efforts have been rebuffed, or people fail to turn up when they've promise to meet up. In those cases, we need to ask God to give us the strength and desire to persevere.

Perceived needs v the most important need

We read this in Mark 2:5–12:

> When Jesus saw their faith, he said to the paralyzed man, 'Son, your sins are forgiven.' Now some teachers of the law were sitting there, thinking to themselves, 'Why does this fellow talk like that? He's blaspheming! Who can forgive sins but God alone?' Immediately Jesus knew in his spirit that this was what they were thinking in their hearts, and he said to them, "Why are you thinking these things? Which is easier: to say to this paralyzed man, 'Your sins are forgiven,' or to say, 'Get up, take your mat and walk'? But I want you to know that the Son of Man has authority on earth to forgive sins.' So he said to the man, 'I tell you, get up, take your mat and go home.' He got up, took his mat and walked out in full view of them all. This

amazed everyone and they praised God, saying, 'We have never seen anything like this!'

This paralysed man was on a mat, unable to move or do anything for himself, which is why his friends lowered him down through the roof. We are not told of his emotional state, but he trusted his friends and they trusted that Jesus could help him. His disability meant that he faced many other issues including poverty and social exclusion. There was no government help or social security benefits. He couldn't get a mobility scooter or a wheelchair, and the government didn't come out to modify his home to make access easier. This man's life was tragic in every way, and yet Jesus looks past the man's temporary struggles and immediate physical needs, to address his most serious and eternal need. This man, his friends and everyone present that day needed to understand that what he needed more than anything else in his life was forgiveness from his sins and to be made right with God.

The teachers of the law who were there should have understood that Jesus' forgiveness of this man's sins was a sign that he is the Messiah, the Son of God, the sinless God-Man. Instead, they accuse Jesus of blasphemy. Jesus, after forgiving the man, now sees to the man's temporary, physical needs and heals him. Then we read that he gets up and walks away. Everyone is amazed and marvels at what Jesus has done.

People never come into our churches and our lives thinking that their biggest need is spiritual. They always come looking for some sort of physical help, or with a need to have their complicated life issues resolved. It is up to us, through the process of evangelism, to educate them about what they *perceive* their need is, and what scripture teaches about what their *real* need is.

The reality is that nobody can earn their forgiveness. We are all as helpless as that paralysed man lying at the feet of Jesus. We can no more forgive our own sins, than he could walk on his own. We are as helpless and dead in our sins, as the man was lying on that mat. All we can do is trust in the word of God and submit to the gospel of God. Do we have faith that Jesus can forgive all those that come before him?

There is no forgiveness if we don't preach the gospel when the lost seek us out.

Evangelising those who don't seek us out

But what about when the lost aren't looking for forgiveness? We need to learn from what Jesus did.

Immediately, after the event with the paralysed man, we read this about how Jesus went out again. This time he was beside the sea, and a large crowd of people came to him, and he was teaching them (Mk. 2:13).

Once again, Jesus is surrounded by crowds of people who had come to see him. This verse shows us how Jesus *intentionally* goes to a public place, by the sea, so that he could teach them the good news. Many of the people at this place hadn't sought him out. They were busy trying to earn a living – fishermen selling their catch at markets and people who had travelled for miles to trade. Yet, Jesus comes among them and begins to evangelise. This is what he does. He seeks out unbelievers in the community, by going to places where they hang out, and speaks into their lives.

Taking the gospel out

Many churches in the UK are thinking of ways to attract people through the doors of their building. They put on all kinds of events to try to attract the local community. We do it at my own church as we put on lots of different activities in the hope of getting people through the doors. This is good. We need to do all we can to make our churches attractive to the lost, and pray that they would visit us and seek us out.

But we also need to remember that, on its own, this approach isn't enough. For every person that visits us there are many more that don't. In these cases, we must leave our warm buildings and seek out the lost.

For many years, our church didn't own a building, and I found it to be very frustrating and limiting. However, as time went on, I began to appreciate it as a blessing in disguise because it forced us into our local community. It meant that we had to go to the places where people congregated, like the local library. These weren't places we would have gone had we had our own building. But, as we used the facilities for children's clubs and other evangelistic events, the gospel began to spread. Being forced to meet in different public spaces meant that we constantly ran into unbelievers on a regular basis.

Like Jesus, we went to where the locals hung out. We began to intentionally seek out those who weren't looking for us. They were as surprised by us as we were by them, but the upshot was loads of new friendships and amazing opportunities to evangelise that would not have happened if we'd had a static building.

In our own communities we need to be looking out for the public places people meet. Instead of hiding in our building, let's go out to meet people, build relationships and proclaim the gospel. What clubs can we start or join, what hobbies have we got, where can we socialise and hang out to meet new people?

If we want to see the lost reached with the gospel, we need to be like Jesus and intentionally look for those who aren't looking for us, as we take the gospel out.

Evangelising those who don't look like us

In Mark 2:14–15 we read:

> As he walked along, he saw Levi son of Alphaeus sitting at the tax collector's booth. 'Follow me,' Jesus told him, and Levi got up and followed him. While Jesus was having dinner at Levi's house, many tax collectors and sinners were eating with him and his disciples, for there were many who followed him.

Levi is almost certainly another name for Matthew, one of Jesus' first disciples. He was a tax collector, employed by the Romans, and a hated member of the Jewish community. His own people viewed him as a traitor and he was rejected by everyone, except fellow tax men.

Yet Jesus chooses him to be a follower and disciple, someone who will go on to write the Gospel of Matthew. In doing this,

Evangelism

Jesus demonstrates to us that he chooses the unexpected, the unlikely, the unliked and the unloved.

Because of this, Levi hears the voice of Jesus and obeys his command to follow him. He literally gets up and walks away from his job and his whole way of life. He gives up a profitable money-making scam to follow the Lord. Interestingly, Jesus recruits from within a group of people that nobody really wants to associate with.

In verse 15, we see how Jesus brought different groups of people together. We see the relationship between Jesus and Levi, Levi and his mates, Jesus and his disciples, and Jesus and the lost, the sinners and the rejected. People who were ordinarily strangers were united through their friendship with Jesus. Like the friends of the disabled man, Levi was buzzing about meeting Jesus – and he wanted to introduce his mates to him. We see Jesus and his disciples socialising with the local community, many of whom were seen as outcasts and sinners. They were having food, chilling out, relaxing, having fun and being friends to those who probably didn't have many.

Building long term, genuine relationships

At our church, we have had some fantastic outreach events. We've had carol services that attracted 90 unbelievers. Every week at our football outreach we meet with 15 unbelievers. At our mums and toddlers' group, 30 unbelievers attend. These are big numbers (for us at least) and they make us feel great and so we post them in our newsletters and funding bids. However, the reality is, as good and as excited as it makes us feel, high attendance at our events is pointless without conversions.

Where we see the real fruit is with the personal relationships we've built up, when we meet someone for a coffee, have someone round for lunch, or are just chatting with a neighbour over the garden fence. This isn't as exciting as a big event. It requires patience and hard work, but this is where we see the real fruit over the long term.

The kind of fruit that comes, for example, from us investing years talking to the local hairdresser, who gets saved, and now runs an evangelistic Bible study for interested clients in her salon. Or from spending years supporting a single mum from a homeless hostel and having her and the children round for tea. From spending years meeting with a man for breakfast and then having the opportunity to share the gospel and pray with him just hours before his death.

It is important for Christians to spend time together as a church, but we also need be spending time in the community. We need to prioritise spending time with people, building relationships – and genuine friendships rather than running large events.

Relationships that are built in the home, in the car, in the pub and at the gym, living life together with our neighbours and loving them by introducing them to Jesus are such an important part of evangelism in our schemes and estates.

If we want to see the lost reached with the gospel, then we need to be like Jesus and love and befriend those who are maybe on the fringes of our communities.

Spending time with sinners

Who are the people in our communities, and what can we do to reach out to them evangelistically?

In Mark 2:16–17 we read:

> When the teachers of the law who were Pharisees saw him eating with the sinners and tax collectors, they asked his disciples: 'Why does he eat with tax collectors and sinners?' On hearing this, Jesus said to them, 'It is not the healthy who need a doctor, but the sick. I have not come to call the righteous, but sinners.'

We are all spiritually sick. The Pharisees were the religious leaders, experts in the law of God. In an effort to obey God, they devised hundreds of extra rules to help keep people from sinning. A lot of these religious men looked, superficially at least, very godly. Because they kept religiously to their own rules, they looked down on others who they viewed as more sinful than them. What they failed to realise was that they needed the forgiveness of Jesus as much as the tax collectors and others in society whom they looked down upon.

They refused to accept that they were as sinful as every other sinner. They were the opposite of Jesus. They kept themselves to themselves because they didn't want to be polluted by sinners. They would never dream of being seen in public with a tax collector, never mind going to a party full of them. They were convinced, mistakenly, that not only were they better than anyone else, but that God viewed them favourably because of their self-righteousness.

Some of them even looked down on Jesus and were mortified that a rabbi would eat at the home of a person like Levi. That's why they ask Jesus' disciples what he was up to at the end of verse 16. Their question wasn't really a question – it was a statement of condemnation. In their worldview, if Jesus is hanging around with the unclean and the sinners, then he must be just as unclean and sinful.

How much of our social time is spent with sinners? Are there particular people that we avoid, or look down upon? Are we honest about our own self-righteousness?

One of the key signs of spiritual vitality and maturity is that we view ourselves correctly. Maybe we don't take drugs. Maybe we don't fall down drunk at parties. Maybe we are not sexually promiscuous. Yet, that doesn't mean we are any better than others, just because our sins may be below the surface, or are kept within the privacy of our own home.

The fact is we are all sick with sin, we are all born rejecting God, we are all rebels at heart, and we all need a spiritual doctor. This is true whether we are a respectable business owner, a schoolteacher, retired, or unemployed. The fact is that, regardless of social status, the only person who can cure our sin sickness is Jesus.

The scandal of grace

Because God is holy, he simply can't let sin go unpunished. As sinners, we all deserve to be condemned by God, and our only hope of peace and reconciliation with our Creator is through repentance and faith in Jesus alone. From Adam and Eve in

Eden, every person that has ever lived has sinned. Everyone that is, except Jesus. He is the sinless Son of God who gave up the riches of glory in order to enter into our reality.

He was hated and persecuted because of the truth he taught and the compassion he showed toward those on the fringes of society. He devoted his life to obeying the Father, instead of choosing to do his own thing. He never sinned. He was constantly rejected. He was abused. He was assaulted. He was falsely accused of crimes. He was convicted by an unlawful court. He was murdered on a cross. He took the punishment that we all deserve for rebelling against God. In fact, as he died on the cross, he was facing the full wrath of the Father poured out upon him. He who knew no sin, was made sin. He died. He rose again three days later, having conquered sin and defeating death

This means that anyone who trusts in him can be forgiven and know eternal life, regardless of whether we like them or not, or whether we think they deserve it or not. That is the scandal of God's grace.

But there is more. Jesus ascended to heaven, where he sits at the right hand of the Father, praying constantly for his people. He will return one day for his church, for everyone who trusts and follows him, and when he does so he will make everything new.

There will be no more sin or sadness or death or pain or suffering.

That's the gospel we need to preach to our own self-righteous hearts, long before we preach it to others. We need to remind one another constantly that we are no better than the sinners we are evangelising.

Conclusion

For those of us who don't know Jesus as Lord and Saviour, we need to know that Jesus is ready to meet us where we are right now. The only thing we need to do to be saved, is to respond to the good news in repentance and faith.

We need to stop trying to please God. We cannot please him outside of Jesus.

We need to trust in his perfect life, death and resurrection. We need to turn away from our old rebellious life of doing things our way and begin doing things his way.

If we are Christians, then we need to be ready to preach the gospel *when the lost seek us out*. But we must also be prepared to go out and evangelise the lost who have no intention of seeking us out. We need to evangelise *all* people, even those we would rather not associate with. We need to think of evangelism less as hit-and-miss events (which might be useful) and more in terms of building genuine friendships over a long period of time (which will definitely be useful). We should rejoice in what Jesus has done for us, despite our sin, and use that as the fuel to do all we can to introduce others to him. We must become more and more like Jesus, the true friend of sinners.

3. The cost of discipleship

Matthew Spandler-Davison
Acts29 VP Global Outreach and 20schemes
Senior Director

In 1945, Romania was invaded by Communist soldiers. They swiftly seized control of the country and immediately began to crack down on churches. Pastor Richard Wurmbrand (1909–2001) was an evangelical minister in Romania. He is widely recognised as one of the country's greatest Christian leaders, authors and teachers. After the invasion of 1945, Wurmbrand began a vigorous 'underground' ministry to oppressed Christians. He also courageously sought to reach out to the Russian soldiers occupying his country. Perhaps unsurprisingly, he was arrested in 1948 and spent three years in solitary confinement, seeing only his Communist torturers. He was transferred to a group cell, where the torture continued for five more years. Listen to what he said about that moment:

> It was strictly forbidden to preach to other prisoners. It was understood that whoever was caught doing this received a

> severe beating. Several of us decided to pay the price for the privilege of preaching, so we accepted [the Communists'] terms. It was a deal; we preached, and they beat us. We were happy preaching. They were happy beating us, so everyone was happy.[1]

How could he find such extraordinary courage and where did his sense of determination to press on in the work of the gospel come from? Well, he tells us,

> Did I believe in God? Now the test had come. I was alone. There was no salary to earn, no golden opinions to consider. God offered me only suffering – would I continue to love Him?[2]

What does it mean to be a disciple of Jesus Christ? What is a life of service, devotion and worship of Jesus meant to be like? Are there super Christians like Wurmbrand who sacrifice and do the hard things – and then the rest of us? Does God demand the same kind of radical, selfless, resolute faith from each one of us?

20schemes exists to make disciples in the places where life can be hard. Where ministry can often be lonely and thankless. Where there is often an overwhelming indifference and outright hostility to the gospel. Why do we do it? Because Christ commands us to go and make disciples. Even in the hard places. That is our mission.

---

[1] Richard Wurmbrand, *Tortured for Christ,* Hodder & Stoughton, 2004.
[2] Richard Wurmbrand, *In God's Underground,* Living Sacrifice Book Company, 2004.

The cost of discipleship

The sad truth is that followers of Jesus like Wurmbrand are hard to find in many of our churches. We say we are a disciple of Jesus, but many of us are content to follow him so long as it doesn't disrupt our comfortable and neat lives. That is not the vision of discipleship that the Bible presents. Discipleship, according to Jesus, involves being willing to set everything aside to make much of Jesus.

How do we grow men and women in our churches to be truly committed followers of Jesus? Willing to do the hard things, grow in their knowledge of the Lord, resist temptation, serve Jesus faithfully even during frustration, starting churches where there are none?

The truth is, if we are going to see disciples made in the hardest places, then we need to change the way we view discipleship.

Let's turn to Luke 9 to answer that question. A close inspection of this text reveals at least two primary marks of a true disciple of Jesus. I wonder, do these marks describe you?

Mark one of discipleship – self-denial

Jesus says, 'If anyone would come after me, let him deny himself' (Lk. 9:23). If anyone would come after me let him *deny* himself.

The word for 'deny' here literally means, 'to enter into poverty'. It means to give up what we own for the sake of knowing Jesus. It certainly means that we are to be prepared to let go of everything, if that is what Christ demands of us. To deny self is to look at our old, unredeemed, cursed, spiritually dead self and say, *'I'm done with you! You cannot stay with me anymore, for I belong to Jesus now.'*

Our old self-centred self loves to be praised, to be made much of. It loves approval and glory, and comfort and ease. Our old self whispers in our ear, *'It's all about me. Look at me. Make much of me. Make me great. Make my life easy and comfortable.'* But those who deny self say, *'It's all about Jesus. Look at Jesus, Make much of Jesus. Make Jesus great. Make my life hard and uncomfortable for the sake of declaring the worth of Jesus'.*

Another word for this, one that the Bible uses often, is the word 'repentance'. It is a daily denial of our own glory. It is a daily forsaking of our own self-centred desires. The heart of discipleship is pursuing a deepening relationship with Jesus. It is having a growing desire to serve him and to put him first.

This command, 'deny yourself' applies to everyone, without exception. We must submit ourselves to the will and the word of God. But, if we are honest, we find this kind of talk so difficult to hear in a culture that celebrates and worships self. Personal pride is seen as an attractive trait. We are programmed, from birth, to chase pleasure, material comfort and security. We are encouraged to deny ourselves nothing.

We live in a time unlike any other. Everyone has a platform. Everyone has an audience. At the click of a button, we can broadcast our carefully curated experiences to an audience of friends and followers. How can we deny self in a selfie world? But Jesus is clear in Luke 9 that if we want to follow him, then he must become the central focus of our lives. Christianity is not about us. It's all about Jesus. We must deny ourselves and follow him.

Mark two of discipleship: sacrifice

The second mark of a genuine disciple of Jesus is that of sacrifice. Not just being willing to let go but also being willing to endure hardship. We let go of comforts and accept discomfort for the sake of Jesus. Look at verse 23 again. Jesus tells us to *take up our cross daily* and follow him.

Remember that Jesus is talking directly to his disciples here. Peter has just confessed that Jesus is the Messiah in verse 20. In response to this Jesus reveals to them what kind of Messiah he was going to be. 'The Son of Man must suffer many things and be rejected by the elders and chief priests and scribes, and be killed, and on the third day be raised' (verse 22).

This was not what they were expecting to hear. It is likely that Peter and the disciples believed that to follow Jesus would mean more wealth, power, fame and fortune for them. These men thought they had a deal with Jesus. They give up their careers, their homes, and their families to follow him now, they enter momentary pain and discomfort, because he will lead them in a glorious revolution that would mean political power and prestige in their future. It seemed like a reasonable deal to strike. But Jesus corrects their thinking. In a sense, he is telling them to, 'Follow me and deny yourself and be prepared to experience ongoing suffering, sacrifice and hardship.'

Jesus is clear in Luke 9:23–27 that those who follow him are following him into suffering. It is a costly path. For some, it is a deadly path. For all of us, it is a daily act of cross-bearing. We can never overestimate the humiliation of dying on the cross. It was a punishment set aside for the worst of the worst. It was a shameful and terrifying way to die. Jesus is telling them – and us – that if you want to follow me, you will suffer opposition, shame, persecution, even death for my sake. That is the price. That is the cost. It's war. That is what it means to be a Christ follower.

Jesus is not a beggar who is pleading with us, 'Oh come and follow me so that I might make you happy and your life easier.' He is not a beggar who is pleading, but a King who is commanding us to follow him into the battle for his glory. He never promises that the way of following him will be easy. But he does promise that he will help us and he will never forsake us.

Do you remember what Satan offered Jesus in the wilderness in Matthew 4? When Jesus was being tempted by Satan, he was being offered glory without the cross. '*Look at all you can have, Jesus, you can have fame, fortune, power, if you follow me.*' Satan offered Jesus wealth without the cross, he offered him power without the cross, he offered him comfort and ease without sacrifice. That is always the lie of Satan.

That same lie is being thrown at us every day of every week. It's the lie that says, '*This life is all about you, you can be great, you can have ease, you can be made much of, you can be comfortable, you can be celebrated.*'

When our life becomes painful and difficult, we start to shake our fist at God! But Jesus comes and says, 'No! Do not

The cost of discipleship

buy the lie, follow me, deny yourself, and if you do, then know what it means. It means giving up your comfort, your ease, your popularity, your fortune. This isn't going to be easy. Satan and the entire world are opposed to us in this. It will mean you taking up your cross daily, being mocked, ridiculed, shamed, humiliated and attacked – all because of me.'

Sounds good, doesn't it? Who's up for that?

The truth is this can get really hard. Staying the course, remaining faithful, forsaking self, serving Jesus, it's not easy. We need to stop making false promises to people that if they follow Jesus their life will get easier. Being a disciple is a daily battle. We live in a land and time that is increasingly hostile to Jesus.

What we believe, how we behave, what we value – it is at odds with the world around us. Even the idea of planting a church or going to a church is considered offensive to some in our communities. These days, to be a follower of Jesus is to be told that we are hateful, that we are bigoted, that we are intolerant, that our views are unacceptable, that what we stand for is disgusting to this so-called progressive, twenty-first-century reality.

We are told that to trust the Bible is to trust something that is from the Dark Ages. We are told that to pray is to be weak and to believe in fairy tales. We are told that to believe in the sanctity of life, in the sanctity of marriage, in the biblical idea of love and justice is at odds with what it means to be British. Teachers, nurses, doctors, pastors, business owners, parents

– each day our faith is being challenged and each day we are being more and more marginalised.

The world that our children will grow up in will be no less hostile to the gospel. Indeed, it will likely be far more hostile. They may be overlooked for job offers simply because they belong to a Bible-believing church. Some may become poor because of their faith. How do we prepare them for that? How do we as believers deal with that in our own life?

To believe what we believe is utterly scandalous in this country today, it flies in the face of all that this world believes, it provokes the anger and scorn of people all around us. But it has always been this way. We are not playing a game; we are fighting a war. To believe the Bible and to call people to faith in Jesus, to live a life of service to Jesus, and to forsake worldly desires has always set the people of God on a collision course with the world.

Calvin put it this way, 'All things around us are in opposition to God's promises ... What then is to be done? We must ... pass by ourselves and all things connected with us, that nothing may hinder or prevent us from believing that God is true.'[3]

Therefore, we need one another. To carry each other's burdens. To keep us from wandering. To keep our eyes fixed on Jesus. To pick us up when we stumble. It is why you can't be a follower of Jesus apart from the church of Jesus. We need each other.

---

[3] John Calvin, *Commentary on Romans*. Available at: https://ccel.org/ccel/calvin/calcom38.viii.x.html. Accessed 22/05/2023.

So, what does this mean for us? The German Protestant pastor, Dietrich Bonhoeffer, wrote 'When Christ calls a man, He bids him come and die.'[4]

Jesus expects that we who belong to him will be men and women who are willing to be opposed, to be shamed, to suffer, and to die – all for him. Disciples of Jesus will take up their cross daily – even if that means walking into suffering and sacrifice. Martin Luther, when he came to Christ, said that he realised 'this grace had cost him his very life, and must continue to cost him the same price day by day.'[5]

Jesus knows that what he is asking of us seems impossible. This way of living can be brutal, hard, and relentless. Yet we are so weak, and too often lack courage. Jesus presents two compelling arguments as to why what he is calling us to is in fact for our good.

Motivation one for disciples: keep eternity in view

It may sound surprising but a self-denying, cross-taking life is in fact the only way to truly find life – and the most glorious of lives at that.

Why would we do this, what would lead us to deny ourselves and be willing to suffer shame, humiliation and opposition? What would motivate us to give up ease and comfort? Luke 9 goes on: 'For whoever would save his life will lose it, but whoever loses his life for my sake will save it. For what does it

---

4 Dietrich Bonhoeffer, *The Cost of Discipleship*, Broadman & Holman, 1998, p. 99.

5 Quoted in Bonhoeffer, *The Cost of Discipleship*, p. 49.

profit a man if he gains the whole world and loses or forfeits himself?' (Lk. 9:24-25).

This self-denying, cross-taking life is the only way to save our souls. Everything around us is dying. We are dying. Everything around us is corrupt. We are corrupt. There is sin and darkness, sickness, disease, hatred and death. There is no getting away from it. *The wages of sin is death*. We are condemned and under a curse.

Most people around us are trying their utmost to live their best life here and now. From time to time, they can appear happy and content. But that doesn't change the reality that all people apart from God are condemned and on their way to an eternal hell.

Even terminally sick people can have good days – but that doesn't change the fact that their condition is terminal. Our condition is terminal. Jesus gives us a reality check. You think that your comfort and your ease and your popularity and your wealth are good right now? They might feel good now, but there will come a day when they will all be gone and then what will you be left with?

Jesus is setting out the terms of this arrangement for us: You can have it all now and lose it forever OR You can give it up now and gain it forever. Because 'what does it profit a man to gain the whole world and forfeit his soul?' There is nothing to be gained from pursuing the world and avoiding the self-denying, cross-taking life of following Jesus.

You may say this life of following Jesus is just too hard. I want to go back to following my friends, my lusts and my desires. You hear the call of the world seducing you back into its ways and you may think that maybe your life would be simpler or easier if you weren't following Jesus. There is nothing to be gained there but everything to lose. To avoid this life of self-denial and cross-taking is a deadly gamble. You can be the wealthiest man on earth and yet remain utterly bankrupt before a holy God. Likewise, you can be the poorest man on earth and yet own it all as a co-heir with Christ.

There will come a day when you and I will die. On that day we will stand before our Creator and there is no amount of wealth, no human accolades, no worldly trophies, no degrees, no sports success, no career title, no number of friends that will shield you from the wrath of God who calls on you to deny yourself and follow Jesus! Disciples are eternally minded. Their eyes are fixed on the prize set before them.

Motivation two for disciples: Jesus is Coming

> For whoever is ashamed of me and of my words, of him will the Son of Man be ashamed when he comes in his glory and the glory of the Father and of the holy angels. But I tell you truly, there are some standing here who will not taste death until they see the kingdom of God (Lk. 9:26–27).

This is the second reason why a self-denying cross-taking life is in fact the best of lives – because on that last day, Christ will be ashamed of those who were ashamed of him. How utterly tragic and terrifying that will be.

Jesus says to us, 'You want to be a disciple, you want to gain eternal life? Then treasure me above all else. Treasure me above the promise of riches, and comfort and accolades, and praise and approval. Treasure me above anything that this dying and God-denying world has to offer you. Don't be ashamed of me when the opposition comes. Don't be ashamed of me when the ridicule comes.'

George Whitefield, the great English preacher, wrote in the 1700s, 'In our days, to be a true Christian is to be a scandal.'[6] How true that is for us in this day.

To the person who refuses to take up his cross, Jesus says, 'When I come on that day, I will be ashamed of you.' How utterly tragic that will be. What a wasted life. This is about glory – about who will be glorified in your life. Every day that we cast off our sinful desires, every day that we fight against temptation, every day we resist the world and seek to serve Jesus, we aren't doing so simply so we can be a better person. We are doing it because we believe that Jesus is the better man, and that he is worthy of the sacrifice.

He laid down his life for us. He emptied himself. He took upon himself our shame and our guilt when he took up his cross. How then can we do anything other than to serve him?

Follow Jesus even if it means taking up the cross and experiencing temporary suffering now. We do so because Jesus is worthy of glory.

---

[6] George Whitefield, 'The Necessity and Benefits of Religious Society'. Available at: https://ccel.org/ccel/whitefield/sermons.x.html. Accessed 22/05/2023.

The cost of discipleship

Take time to really consider the unimaginable glory that awaits those who follow Jesus. 'For whoever is ashamed of me and of my words, of him will the Son of Man be ashamed when he comes in his glory and the glory of the Father and of the holy angels' (Lk. 9:26). Jesus is coming again, and he will come in his glory, his power and his majesty. The angels will come and will declare his glory.

The church gets a taste, a mere fleeting glimpse, of glory as we walk with Jesus together in this dark and treacherous world. The longer we follow Jesus the more our affections for him grow. But there is a day coming when the fog of war will clear and we will see clearly, brilliantly, the full majesty of God's glory and we will say, 'It is well with my soul'!

Soon after his release from captivity Pastor Wurmbrand and his wife founded *Voice of the Martyrs* to minister to Christians who are daily taking up their cross and suffering persecution all over the world. They travelled throughout the world to provide relief to families of imprisoned Christians in Islamic nations, Communist nations, and other countries where Christians are persecuted because of their faith.

> In spiritual matters, the only real glory is in the renunciation of glorifying self. 'For to me, to live is Christ, and to die is gain' (Phil. 1:21).
> 'Do not fear those who kill the body but cannot kill the soul' (Mt. 10:28).'
> Worms, fire, or the sea might consume my body. But my spirit will live in a world with no more wanderings and trials. I do

not have to pass through many painful incarnations. Beyond death lies paradise.[7]

If we are to be healthy, growing, vibrant disciples of Jesus, if we are to see healthy churches in our communities, especially in the hard places, then it will mean being followers of Jesus who are self-denying, cross-taking, eternally minded, resolutely confident disciples.

We are to plant and be a part of churches where men and women are being daily challenged to be willing to follow Jesus regardless of the cost. Let us commit to do that work of making disciples, so that Christ might be worshipped where he is not worshipped.

---

[7] Richard Wurmbrand, *The Oracles of God,* Voice of The Martyrs, 2016.

4. Worship in the schemes: Learning to lament

Sol Fenne
Musical Director for 20schemes

lament, noun: *a passionate expression of grief or sorrow, or a complaint; song, poem or piece of music expressing grief, regret or mourning;* **verb:** *to express passionate grief, regret or disappointment about something.*

The downward spiral

'We've been looking everywhere for you, Chris! What have you taken?'

Chris didn't respond. He was a small lad for his age and he stayed slouched on the kerb as we approached him. He had his hood up and he was clutching his stomach. He could barely keep his eyes open and tears were streaming down his face. He was in a bad way.

'Can we get an ambulance down here, please?'

Chris was only a child, barely a teenager, and yet that morning he had found as many pills as he could in his flat, stolen a load more from a local petrol station and taken them all.

'I just want to die,' he told me.

Earlier that day his mum had reported him missing and I was one of the police officers tasked with finding him. When tracing missing persons, part of the initial routine enquiries includes attending the home address to get as much information as possible to help in the search: physical description, when and where they were last seen, known associates, other addresses or places he was known to frequent, and, if possible, a recent photo. I remember the photo his mum gave me because it was such a nice photo, taken only a few years before, of Chris with his little sister and mum on holiday. He was holding a parrot and had an innocent and cocky grin on his face. They all looked so happy. He looked so young.

What had happened?

Chris had become a heroin addict. Usually, lads like Chris regarded junkies as the lowest of the low – yet here he was, hopelessly trapped.

Chris had no aspirations, no-one encouraged him to have any. He may have had a nice holiday once, but the reality was he was growing up in a tough scheme in the west of Edinburgh which is notorious for violence and drugs. His dad had abandoned the family a few years before, his mum was trying her best with him but was struggling to cope as he became more and more angry and abusive towards her and his younger sister. He had just been kicked out of school and had started getting into trouble with the police. For youngsters like Chris, there's not really any good reason to not try drugs, they're easy to get and they offer escape at first from the reality that there's nothing good on the horizon. Chris' lament was a hopeless one, his lostness was driving him into despair, his young life was spiralling downwards, deeper and deeper into the darkness. To him, death seemed to be the only answer.

> For these things I weep;
> My eyes overflow with tears;
> For a comforter is far from me
> One to revive my spirit
> My children are desolate,
> For the enemy has prevailed (Lam. 1:16).

The Fall: our problems are worse than we think

There is much to lament in the schemes of Scotland. As a country, it remains the drug death capital of Europe and many here are born into, live with and die in endless cycles of abuse, family dysfunction and addiction. As painful and soul-crushing as that is, Chris – and all those like him – have far greater problems than they think. There is something worse than heroin addiction. There is something worse than being abandoned by a parent. There is something worse than going hungry at night. There is something worse than feeling that life is not worth living.

God is at war with us.

We are rebels against our Holy Creator. We refuse to bow the knee to him in repentance and faith. We refuse to recognise his right to rule our lives. We refuse to recognise Jesus as our Lord and Saviour – as the Lord and Saviour. Because of this, he is at war with us and his holy wrath rests upon us from the moment we are born until the moment we die.

That's not the way it was meant to be.

Romans 1 tells us we were wonderfully and fearfully created in God's image to have a relationship with him. But, instead, we've exchanged the truth about God for a lie and worshipped and served created things rather than the Creator. We are more interested in ourselves than in the One who made us. We've become futile in our thinking, and our foolish hearts have been darkened (Rom. 1:21–25). In our sin, we cannot approach the throne of God as he reigns in all purity and holiness and righteousness and eternal glory.

- We were made to live for him – but instead, we live for ourselves
- We were created to worship him – but instead, we worship ourselves
- We were made to find fulfilment in him – but instead, we seek to find it in ourselves and others
- We were created to walk with him – but instead, we hide from him.

Not long after the sin of Adam and Eve in Genesis 3:9–10, God calls out to Adam in the Garden of Eden, "'Where are you?"

And he said, "I heard the sound of you in the garden, and I was afraid, because I was naked, and I hid myself."

Chris's physical and mental problems mask his deeper, spiritual ones. He is cut off from God. He is a rebel against his Creator. He is under God's holy wrath. He will never find the peace he wants in anything or anybody else.

His problems are far bigger than he realises.

Satan: our cunning enemy

We have an enemy of souls, whose goal is to keep us away from Jesus Christ. He wants to blind us to the truth of the good news about Jesus. In fact, he has been very good at blinding the minds of unbelievers to the truths of the Bible. He works to ensure that we don't focus on our souls. He works to keep us focused on the here and now. Paul tells the church in 2 Corinthians 4:4 that, 'the god of this world has blinded the minds of the unbelievers, to keep them from seeing the light of the gospel of the glory of Christ, who is the image of God.'

Satan was present when mankind fell. In fact, his was the voice that questioned God's goodness in the Garden of Eden. It was his lie that caused Adam and Eve to shatter the perfect relationship they enjoyed with their Creator. Satan is a deceiver, and he is just as present and active in our modern world as he was all those millennia ago in that perfect paradise.

Consider the wisdom of Proverbs 7:21–23.

> With much seductive speech she persuades him;
> with her smooth talk she compels him.

> All at once he follows her,
> as an ox goes to the slaughter,
> or as a stag is caught fast
> till an arrow pierces its liver;
> as a bird rushes into a snare;
> he does not know that it will cost him his life.

Satan wants us trapped in the hopeless cycles of addiction. He doesn't care if we're sad or happy. He wants to suck us into the downward spiral of dark godlessness. He wants us to suffer.

Satan is happy if we are on medication for depression. He is happy if we feel alone and helpless. He is happy if we feel cut off from the world. He is happy if we don't feel that people truly understand us. He is happy if we commit suicide. He is happy if we end up in jail or on the streets. He is happy if we complain about our lot in life. He is happy if we are bitter about the things that have happened to us. He is happy if we cannot get past our childhood traumas. He is happy to keep us in an abusive relationship.

But he is not happy if we begin to lament. Really lament. Biblically lament.

Biblical lamenting ...

Satan is not happy if we lament our fallen-ness. He doesn't care that we lament the sorrows of this world, as long as we remain spiritually blind to our own lost-ness. He doesn't want us to lament that we are dead in our sin. He doesn't want us to know there is One who longs to hear our cries. He doesn't want us

Worship in the schemes

to relate to the One who is ready and who has done everything necessary to restore hopelessly blind rebels to himself. He doesn't want us to seek the One who loves the outcast and who pursues the wayward.

Satan doesn't want us to biblically lament. He doesn't want us to pray like the Psalmist in Psalm 130:1-2. 'Out of the depths I cry to you, O Lord! O Lord, hear my voice! Let your ears be attentive to the voice of my pleas for mercy!' He doesn't want us to cry out to the man of sorrows. He doesn't want you to cry out to Jesus in repentance and faith. If we are ever going to cry out to the great physician, we need to know he's there, that he loves us and that we're sick. We need him to diagnose our problem.

It is only then that our crying in the darkness becomes a *true lament* that reaches heavenwards to the very throne of the living God.

We can only cry out from the depths to the Lord because he first descended from his throne in glory, down into the pit where we are. He came to us, to reveal himself to us and to rescue us from our sin and from the grip of Satan's deception. Christ's willing descent into this fallen world culminated in the cross where, just before he died, he cried the darkest lament that has and ever will be uttered in all eternity:

> 'Eli, Eli, lema sabachthani?' that is, 'My God, my God, why have you forsaken me?' (Mt. 27:46)

His lament at this moment was the tormented cry of our Saviour who faced separation from the Father in order that we might be reconciled to our Creator. Our laments in this life, even our faintest cries for help, are now heard by the Almighty King of Kings because he walks by our side along the way, possible only because we have been made right with him through Christ.

> Since then we have a great high priest who has passed through the heavens, Jesus, the Son of God, let us hold fast our confession. For we do not have a high priest who is unable to sympathise with our weaknesses, but one who in every respect has been tempted as we are, yet without sin. Let us then with confidence draw near to the throne of grace, that we may receive mercy and find grace to help in time of need (Heb. 4:14-16).

Biblical lamenting ... is a lifelong reality for all Christians

Is there anything more wonderful than seeing somebody come to saving faith in Jesus? In the churches planted through 20schemes, we have been privileged to witness the life-transforming power of the gospel many times over the years – evidence before our eyes that God really does pluck people from darkness and bring them into the light. I have seen men and women I thought were hopelessly lost be radically changed, saved from lives of chaos, abuse, and family dysfunction into the family of God.

These are wonderful moments, when a sinner has their burden removed at the cross and experiences for the first time that lightness of foot, that peace which surpasses all understanding, that clear vision of Jesus and that freedom from condemnation. I find it convicting to see the childlike joy and excitement of a new believer. I wish I had that sparkle all the time, but often I don't. Our souls are safe in Christ, our eternity is secure, we have been adopted, but *we're not home yet* and, at some point, every believer must be confronted with this hard truth: *biblical lament is a lifelong thing.*

Christian, consider the following:

> Beloved, do not be surprised at the fiery trial when it comes upon you to test you, as though something strange were happening to you. But rejoice insofar as you share Christ's sufferings, that you may also rejoice and be glad when his glory is revealed (1 Pet. 4:12–13).

> In the world you will have tribulation. But take heart; I have overcome the world (Jn. 16:33).

> Put on the whole armour of God, that you may be able to stand against the schemes of the devil. For we do not wrestle against flesh and blood, but against the rulers, against the authorities, against the cosmic powers over this present darkness, against the spiritual forces of evil in the heavenly places (Eph. 6:11–12).

> Behold, I am sending you out as sheep in the midst of wolves … Brother will deliver brother over to death, and the father his child, and children will rise against parents and have them

> put to death, and you will be hated by all for my name's sake (Mt. 10:16, 21–22).

> Be sober-minded; be watchful. Your adversary the devil prowls around like a roaring lion, seeking someone to devour. Resist him, firm in your faith, knowing that the same kinds of suffering are being experienced by your brotherhood throughout the world (1 Pet. 5:8–9).

> Do not be surprised, brothers, that the world hates you (1 Jn. 3:13).

In the Christian life there is still much to lament. All things *haven't yet* been made new. This world is still fallen, Satan is still prowling, and the passions of the flesh still wage war against our souls. (1 Pet. 2:11).

To lament, biblically and reverently, is to continually remember where we came from. Just as the risen Jesus still bears the scars of his suffering, we too must acknowledge the very real pains and sorrows and struggles of this life. We don't need to just pretend they don't exist. We don't need to hide them away. Christian, we are the ones who can speak like James:

> Count it all joy, my brothers, when you meet trials of various kinds, for you know that the testing of your faith produces steadfastness. And let steadfastness have its full effect, that you may be perfect and complete, lacking in nothing (Jas. 1:2–4).

To lament *is* to worship

Lament, then, is a fundamental part of our worship and it must be a part of ordinary, daily existence and communion with God. Lament for our former state should fuel our present and future worship. Lament over the deceptive works of Satan should fuel our dependence on God and make us strive for wisdom and discernment. Lament for our ongoing battles with sin should fuel our lives of daily repentance. Lament for the ongoing battles of our brothers and sisters in Christ should fuel our commitment to a local church. Lament for the lost should fuel our evangelism.

We long for that day

Christian, we can lament now with an assurance and expectancy of things to come that gives us a joyful perspective of the fleetingness of this life and the temporary nature of our sin here on earth. Our cries to God amidst the raging wars of this life are coming to an end because there is coming a day soon when there'll be no more reason to lament – when we are finally in Christ's presence with all the saints through history who battled and lamented their way through the Christian life, to win the inheritance that is imperishable, undefiled, and unfading (1 Pet. 1:4).

We will stand there in the company of the martyrs who were burnt at the stake, with the early Christians who were fed to the lions in the Colosseum. Those who lived out their lives in prison for their faith. There will be those who were widows and orphans and the countless unborn children who never got the chance to see the light of day here on earth. There will be those who battled depression, who were hated by their families, who were rejected by their friends. All the evangelists who were spat at in the street, all the missionaries who gave their lives proclaiming that Jesus died and rose, all those who battled privately in prayer every day for the lost around them.

One day soon we will all be united and restored and we will all see clearly, even the Lamb who was slain, and we will fall before him and worship him with thanksgiving, reverence and awe for eternity. On that day our lament will be over.

> O God of our salvation
> We long to see the day
> When grief not worth comparing
> Will all be swept away
>
> Our momentary struggle
> And temporary pain
> Will finally be over
> When Jesus comes again
>
> Jesus will return in glory
> So, we take heart, we take heart
> Joyful ending to this story
> So, we take heart, we take heart![1]

---

[1] Sol Fenne, 'Take Heart' from *Hymns In Hard Places,* 20schemes music, 2022. All rights reserved. CCLI #7189146.

5. Prayer

Chris Davidson
Pastor, Merkinch Free Church, Inverness, Scotland

I think we would all agree that the past few years have been unlike what many of us have ever experienced in our lifetime. The banking crisis in 2007, Covid-19 and the war in Ukraine which to date has seen nearly 8 million people flee their homeland.[1] All these troubles in the world, not to mention our own fears, anxieties and hurts. Life can be overwhelming, right?

We can feel smothered by all that is going on in the world and our own situation. We can feel like a weight on our chest is just slowly pushing in on us and we need to take deep breaths because of the stress we are in.

So, it is appropriate for us to look at prayer.

---

1 Ukraine Refugee Situation, UNKCR Operational Data Portal, 25 January 2023, https://data.unhcr.org/en/situations/ukraine. Accessed 22/05/2023.

Prayer – as essential as breathing

If we're training our bodies to be fit, the lungs are essential. If we were to lift a considerable weight, for example, we'd naturally take a deep breath beforehand. Anyone who has run 100 metres breathes heavily as they try to hit their goal, and in our spiritual life prayer is not unlike the respiratory system. It makes us fit and it enables us to endure.

In our prayer lives, we need to breathe in the sweet gospel air from the cross, the life-giving air from the atonement, knowing that we were once dead in our sins but that death and sin have been undone and destroyed by the work of Jesus, knowing that today we stand born again into a living hope. We breathe in the air of new life of newness itself as 2 Corinthians 5 puts it: 'Therefore, if anyone is in Christ, he is a new creation. The old has passed away; behold, the new has come (2 Cor. 5:17).

Prayer is a mark of our new reality and relationship that we've been brought into. But not only that, prayer is essential for our Christian walk and well-being, for building us up and making us fit. As we breathe in the goodness of the gospel, we must also exhale in faith and trust in the Lord.

If we think of prayer as being as essential as breathing, it can help us understand Paul's words in 1 Thessalonians 5, 'Rejoice always, pray without ceasing, give thanks in all circumstances; for this is the will of God in Christ Jesus for you' (1 Thes. 5:16–18).

If we see prayer as the lungs of the soul, then, of course, we can pray without ceasing and always rejoice because every

Prayer

breath is a gift from our incredible Saviour, every prayer a sign of faith and trust in his sovereignty.

Maybe in the past week you have felt spiritually cold and distant from God, and it feels like the battles you face are winning, you're feeling the stress of life pushing down on you, and you feel alone in it all. Have you prayed?

Have you prayed over your fears, pains, stress and hurt?

Maybe you're spiritually suffocating because you have shifted in your dependence on God in prayer and have lost the 'pray without ceasing' Paul encourages us to and replaced it with 'pray when you hit rock bottom'. Some of us could be spiritually suffocating because we have a wrong view of what prayer is and we use prayer like a 'divine Alexa', where we just bark a command and expect it to happen. Or we think that if we could just get the suitable types of words that have power and bring them in prayer, God would hear us, and since we aren't praying right, God isn't hearing us.

To put it simply, prayer is a big deal, and we all need training and encouragement in it. Whether we are a baby Christian or are the oldest pastor in the land, we need to be trained in breathing the good gospel air and exhaling faith, trust and worship. Or as one writer says, to mix my metaphors,

> Prayer is a fine, delicate instrument. To use it right is a great art, a holy art. There is perhaps no greater art than the art of prayer. … The least gifted, the uneducated and the poor can cultivate the holy art of prayer.[2]

---

2 Ole Hallesby, *Prayer*, Augsburg Publishing House, 1931, p. 13.

In other words, we have no excuses not to be training in prayer together.

Therefore, we will get a bit of training in – and Christian training is often an act of remembering, remembering what God has done, and remembering who he is. We often see this kind of training done by God to his people in the Old Testament as he reminds them, 'I am the Lord your God, who brought you out of the land of Egypt' or 'I am the God of your father, the God of Abraham, the God of Isaac, and the God of Jacob' (Ex. 20:2, 3:6).

So, we could say I want to encourage you to remember how to pray – with two simple techniques. The first is to breathe in the goodness of the gospel in prayer. And step two is to breathe out in trust and faith, which is a contrast to the hypocrites and the Gentiles.

Step one: Breathe in

So, step one! Breath in! It sounds so simple but it is crucial for our spiritual health to take a good deep breath in of the gospel in prayer. What I mean by that is reminding yourself of who God is and who you are!

Let's then bring ourselves under the word of God in Matthew 6 as we think about prayer:

> And when you pray, you must not be like the hypocrites. For they love to stand and pray in the synagogues and at the street corners, that they may be seen by others. Truly, I say to you, they have received their reward. But when you pray, go into

your room and shut the door and pray to your Father who is in secret. And your Father who sees in secret will reward you. And when you pray, do not heap up empty phrases as the Gentiles do, for they think that they will be heard for their many words. Do not be like them, for your Father knows what you need before you ask him. Pray then like this:

Our Father in heaven,

hallowed be your name.

Your kingdom come,

your will be done,

on earth as it is in heaven.

Give us this day our daily bread,

and forgive us our debts,

as we also have forgiven our debtors.

And lead us not into temptation,

but deliver us from evil.

For if you forgive others their trespasses, your heavenly Father will also forgive you, but if you do not forgive others their trespasses, neither will your Father forgive your trespasses (Mt. 6:5–15).

Currently, we don't have a TV Licence in our house mainly because I am too tight to pay for a TV licence, but my wife loves watching clips of shows like One Born Every Minute. Or YouTubers who have gone through giving birth. Now, to be honest, I don't like these shows, giving birth is just messy. But there is one moment, in all these clips that I do find grabs my attention. Every time. It's the moment the baby has just popped out and is quickly wrapped up and the midwife rubs its back.

Then the room almost stops moving, time seems to stand still as they all stare and wait.

They do this in the hope of a deep breath from the baby, and once this happens you can see the concern melt away from the professionals' eyes. Because the deep breath is followed by what? A massive cry.

The baby lives. It's ok now. That breath and cry is a good thing! It's reassuring. Is it any wonder then that Jesus in John 3 compares being born to being born again into the household of faith?

Our first action of new birth is usually a deep breath of prayer and a cry of total and utter dependency upon our Lord and God.

We cry Matthew 6, and we say, 'Our Father in heaven'!

We realise who we are, that we are sinners, but now grasping in faith who Christ is. We cry, we pray, we breathe in the wonder that God loved us so much that Christ, being found in human form, humbled himself by becoming obedient to the point of death, even death on a cross (Phil. 2:8).

Prayer is then communion with God our Father through the person of Christ and his work on the cross. Prayer is then a form of spiritual intimacy with our Father in heaven and dependency resting in the character of Christ, who wonderfully made it possible for us to pray. In our training of prayerful people, we need to point them to their salvation and the new life they live.

Tim Keller once tweeted – and it was an excellent tweet – that the only person who dares wake up a king at 3 am for a glass of water is a child. We have that kind of access.

We have that access because of Christ, and our prayers are nothing more than our continued dependency and neediness for our Father, our Christ, our Comforter the Holy Spirit.

Our dependency on prayer and breathing all this gospel goodness isn't just a conversion experience, but is now the state we live in. The cry for help in the war with sin isn't won and done.

Look at verses 11–13 of Matthew 6:

> Give us this day our daily bread,
> and forgive us our debts,
> as we also have forgiven our debtors.
> And lead us not into temptation,
> but deliver us from evil.

This is a daily need. Daily bread is needed, so is daily forgiveness. And daily strength is needed as we wrestle daily with our temptations! We could then say then that prayer is something Christians never graduate from this side of eternity, because it is the lungs of the soul.

The challenge is that in our sinfulness, we want to graduate from dependency. We want to feel self-sufficient; we want to be strong. We, in our sinful pride, want to take the world head-on and win. So being needy, being dependent on our Father in heaven, can be a battle and a daily struggle.

Now hear me here, especially if you are a young believer. You may find it hard to be needy of Jesus. You may find it hard to be dependent in prayer. You may wrongly think, as you look at those 'strong Christians', that they don't battle with sin.

If you think like that, bin it here and now.

Show me a 'strong' Christian and I will show you a prayerful soul – someone who knows that the best way to stand against sin is to be before his Father in prayer.

A strong Christian is someone who often breathes in the goodness of the gospel and who breathes in words like Hebrews 12:

> Therefore, since we are surrounded by so great a cloud of witnesses, let us also lay aside every weight, and sin which clings so closely, and let us run with endurance the race that is set before us, looking to Jesus, the founder and perfecter of our faith, who for the joy that was set before him endured the cross, despising the shame, and is seated at the right hand of the throne of God (Heb. 12:1-2).

So, our first step of training is to remember the goodness of God, his power of salvation and breathe in the sweet gospel air of our dependency on God!

I love a wee book written by a Dutch reformer called O. Hallesby. He says:

> It is not our prayer which draws Jesus into our hearts. Nor is it our prayer which moves Jesus to come into us. All He needs is access. He enters in of His own accord, because He desires to come in. ... To pray is nothing more involved than ... giving Jesus access to our needs and permitting Him to exercise His own power in dealing with them. ... And that requires no

strength. It is only a question of our wills. Will we give Jesus access to our needs?[3]

Will you today? Will you breathe in the gospel in prayer and trust Jesus?

Will you surrender the little strength you have to come before the throne of power in prayer?

Don't swallow the lie that says we must be getting stronger, more capable – as if in some way we outgrow our relationship with God as a child and naturally become more independent into adulthood. In prayer we come as spiritual children, no matter what age we are, with nothing. But we can access the mighty hands of God for our aid.

I heard this story once.

A young boy went to the store with his mother. The shop owner, a kind man, passed him a large jar of boiled sweets and invited him to help himself to a handful. Uncharacteristically, the boy held back. So, the shop owner pulled out a handful for him. When outside, the boy's mother asked why he wouldn't take a handful of sweets when offered. 'Because his hand is much bigger than mine!' said the boy.

Isn't this like prayer? God's hand can carry more than ours, so we pray

> Our Father in heaven,
> hallowed be your name.
> Your kingdom come,
> your will be done,

---

[3] Hallesby, *Prayer*, Augsburg Publishing House, 1931, p. 4–5.

on earth as it is in heaven.

Step one: breathe in the goodness of the gospel.

Step two: Exhale

Step two seems so obvious. What follows a breath in? A breath out, right?

We could say this is the second step to breathing and a natural second step to our prayers too. As we breathe in the goodness of our God, the relationship we now have in him, we become ever more alive for him. We then exhale in faith and trust in our Father in heaven.

It is this pattern that develops us and grows us in our prayer life so that we can say with conviction:

> Your kingdom come,
> your will be done,
> on earth as it is in heaven.

And:

> lead us not into temptation,
> but deliver us from evil.

Let's just pause and take note of what we are praying here because these words are so challenging!

The essence of what this section teaches us is the diminishing of our wills and entrusting all of who we are and what is happening to us to God's sovereign will. In short, exercising faith and trust in God.

Notice that it's '*Your* Kingdom come', highlighting that we have a King who rules and reigns. It's *his* Kingdom, not ours; it is *his* rule, not ours; it is *his* will be done, not ours. Prayer then involves bringing our prayer life in line with the will of God.

How do we do this you may ask? Well, this is where our training kicks in. We need to remember the basics. We need to read our Bibles, we need to learn more about Jesus, we need to pray the Word and apply the Word to our lives so it shapes our prayer life, so that every prayer is God-shaped and God-framed. We can only do this by knowing him in his Word.

We should be so thankful that we don't need to try and figure out these things from a blank page, without God's guidance, because we would slip into what we see so often in the Old Testament – a form of human worship or worshipping the created rather than the creator. But God in his love and grace gave us his whole counsel in the Bible.

If you are wanting to cultivate good prayerfulness in yourself, in our church plants in the schemes, we must cultivate a desire for God's word.

Or as John Newton once wrote.

> How then may the Lord's guidance be expected? In general, He guides and directs His people, by affording them, in answer to prayer, the light of His Holy Spirit, which enables them to understand and to love the Scriptures. The Word of God is not to be used as a lottery, nor is it designed to instruct us by shreds and scraps, which, detached from their proper places, have no determinate import; but it is to furnish us with just principles, right apprehensions to regulate our

judgments and affections, and thereby influence and direct our conduct.[4]

If you are thinking, '*How do I grow in faith and trust in the Lord? How do I develop a healthy second step to my spiritual breathing?*' the answer is we must be people of the Word and prayer. They are linked.

Let's be honest, we cannot manifest trust without experiencing the gospel! That is why breathing in the good news in prayer reminds us that we are saved, loved, healed and forgiven – and breathing out in faith and trust means we can say with conviction

> Your kingdom come,
> your will be done,
> on earth as it is in heaven.

Friends, if you are struggling to trust God, read his Word, read how God never leaves his people or forsakes them, and read the stories of people who trusted God in prayer for their children, their people, their country, their very souls, and read God's response each time he proved that he was to be trusted.

Ask people in your church or church plant how God is answering their prayers, how he can be trusted! Christians shouldn't be panicked by such questions!

But let's be clear today that in Matthew 6, Jesus highlights two groups whose prayers lack trust and faith! Two forms of

---

[4] John Newton, 'On Divine Guidance', *Letters of John Newton,* Banner of Truth Trust, 1869.

prayer we need to avoid and be aware of so that they don't seep into our churches or our own lives.

Look with me again at Matthew 6:5

> And when you pray, you must not be like the hypocrites. For they love to stand and pray in the synagogues and at the street corners, that they may be seen by others. Truly, I say to you, they have received their reward.

Don't be like the hypocrites

They pray in places of worship like the synagogues. They are even bold in prayer, right? By praying at the street corners!

All this isn't for God, Jesus says, but to be seen by others. All to be seen. How good and great they are! How holy and strong a Christian must they be to have faith enough to speak in the street, right? We may think that.

But Jesus is highlighting them because they don't model dependency on God and trust in him. They have no desire to go into a secret place with God and just be themselves and him. That's too exposing and no one would see how great they are.

This small section contrasts the prayer of faith-filled dependence in the Lord's prayer and the hypocrites.

They don't want to pray that God's will would be done, because it fundamentally means they need to decrease so that God may increase!

It reminds me of that parable in Luke 18:9-14:

> [Jesus] also told this parable to some who trusted in themselves that they were righteous, and treated others with contempt [in other words, hypocrites].
>
> 'Two men went up into the temple to pray, one a Pharisee and the other a tax collector. The Pharisee, standing by himself, prayed thus: "God, I thank you that I am not like other men, extortioners, unjust, adulterers, or even like this tax collector. I fast twice a week; I give tithes of all that I get." But the tax collector, standing far off, would not even lift up his eyes to heaven, but beat his breast, saying, "God, be merciful to me, a sinner!" I tell you; this man went down to his house justified, rather than the other.'

The Pharisee who could be seen is the archetype hypocrite. He sees only himself and his own glory, thankful for what he is now in contrast to others. He has no need to breathe in the goodness of the gospel. He has no self-awareness to even see his own will is not the will of God as he judges others. But in contrast, the tax collector is grieved, he is needy, and he is praying that God will accept a sinner like him.

In our prayer life, we breathe out in trust and faith that God's will is the best

> Your kingdom come,
> your will be done,
> on earth as it is in heaven.

I know this is a battle! For me especially, as a church planter, I want things to move, I want that person saved now, I want, I want, but ultimately, I need to surrender in prayer my will and often I remember this quote from Samuel Rutherford, a man who knew a little about battling. He says:

> I pray God that I may never find my will again. Oh, that Christ would subject my will to His, and trample it under His feet. Humility is a strange flower; it grows best in winter weather, and under storms of affliction. I urge you a nearer communion with Christ, and a growing communion.[5]

And that's exactly what the hypocrite runs from in prayer: communion with God!

Don't be like the Gentiles

The second thing to be wary of in prayer that Jesus highlight for us in Matthew 6 is in verse 7-8:

> And when you pray, do not heap up empty phrases as the Gentiles do, for they think that they will be heard for their many words. Do not be like them, for your Father knows what you need before you ask him.

Here Jesus is saying, do not heap up empty phrases. Or for the older generation, don't be babblers in prayer.

Jesus links this type of prayer to the Gentiles. As they had many gods and often their gods were indifferent to them, disconnected from them, angry at them, and they had to be roused to listen. So, think of these wee gods as sitting on their sofa with a warm cuppa and reluctant to move. So, the Gentiles

---

5 I. D. E. Thomas, *A Puritan Golden Treasury*, Banner of Truth Trust, 1977.

used long prayers, repetitive phrases, and words that they thought had power to try and poke and prod their gods into action.

But if we understand prayer, in the language of faith and relationship, then we trust God is active. Just as Jesus says, 'Do not be like them for your Father knows what you need before you ask him.'

God goes before us. He is active, alive and listening. He is proactive – he doesn't need to be woken by our prayers.

But unfortunately, elements of this type of prayer have developed in churches, especially churches I have gone to, where someone will pray for 20 minutes, saying the same thing again and again, maybe in slightly different ways, like God isn't hearing them.

Or some people use bits of the Bible in prayer to grab God's attention because it is his words. Or even using words from the Bible as a type of prayer fairy dust, that if we pray this, God will do it – like praying 'in the name of Jesus Christ of Nazareth'.

Don't miss here me here, it's not wrong to pray God's word back to him. It's not wrong to finish a prayer 'In the name of Jesus, Amen.' But when we see that as a form of invocation, a form of getting God's attention, are we exercising faith and trust, or are we saying that some prayers are heard more clearly by God?

In prayer, let's be wary of what we model. Let's model breathing in the gospel and breathing out in faith and trust. Let's avoid the faithless hypocrite and the trust-less Gentile styles of prayer. This is what will train people in prayer, this is what will train us in prayer because it is so important.

Or as Martin Luther once said: 'To be a Christian without prayer is no more possible than to be alive without breathing.'

6. The church: What is it and why is it so important?

Andy Constable
Pastor, Niddrie Community Church, Edinburgh

I was coming to the end of my studies and the Lord had begun to stir in me a heart to serve in poorer communities. I had read some missionary biographies and I had been on some short-term mission trips and in my arrogance and naivety I thought I knew what I was doing. I would travel to Cape Town with a budget of £500 and turn up in a township and preach the gospel. I would be like the early apostles. However, I was going to do this my way and as far as I was concerned it wouldn't involve the church. The church for me was boring, it hindered the work of the gospel, and I wasn't interested. So, I went off to South Africa to serve and I worked with a ministry that tried to serve young men involved with street gangs and drug addicts. I walked the streets, prayed with people, preached the gospel and worked with lads in this township. We saw four people profess faith and we baptised them.

But the question was now what? What do we do now? We took them along to the white church a few miles down the road, but they robbed the place. We tried taking them out and doing our own stuff during the week, but they were at it during the week – smoking drugs at night and lying to us through the day. It was a mess. That's when I came back to Scotland and Niddrie and I began to see the importance and need of the local church. I began to see why we needed the church, why it was beautiful, and why it was biblical. I began to see it in action in Niddrie and now beyond into other communities.

So, I want to ask this question: Why does local church ministry in poor communities bring glory to God? Why do we insist that local church ministry is the best way to reach the poor? Why is the local church central to God's purposes to reach the poorest people? I want you to see the centrality of the local church and be excited by what God has called you to do in your local church. The church might be small, it might look unimpressive, but it's Christ's and so it's central to God's purposes to reach the poor.

God loves the church

God loves the church. The church is the bride of Christ. Ephesians 5:25 reminds us that Christ laid down his life for the church. Therefore, when churches are *planted* or *revitalised* in the poorest communities it brings glory to God. He loves it because it's establishing his bride. Therefore, if God loves it and the church is his bride, then this is what we should give our time and attention and resources to.

It's like in my marriage to Debbie. She is my wife. I love her. Therefore, she gets my attention, time and resources. I wouldn't be a good husband if I said, 'Do you know what, I'll see you on a Sunday but the rest of the week I'm going to be hanging out with some other ladies in the church and they are going to get my time and attention and resources.' The sister in Christ is my sister not my wife.

Well, the Lord Jesus Christ laid down his life for the church. It's his bride. Therefore, it's the place we should seek to build up. That's the place we should invest our time, attention and resources. And para-churches or mercy ministries exist to build the local church up – not take people, time, and resources away from it.

However, local church ministry has often been sidelined in poor communities because it's often a slow, unglamorous, mundane ministry compared with mercy ministries or para-church ministries where a particular need is met. Let's extend our marriage metaphor – marriage is more complex and difficult than a one-off fling. Why? Because it involves commitment. It involves sacrifice. It involves giving up your rights to serve another. It involves doing life in the mundane. It involves conflict resolution. It involves faithfulness over decades. It's doing the simple things time and again.

It is the same with local church ministry in a scheme. It means moving into that community. It involves discipleship – which is by nature messy. It involves training – which takes time.

We don't often see the results straightaway. It's often boring, unsexy work of living in community, building relationships and sharing the gospel. That's hard to write down on a prayer letter.

Think about the early church in Acts 2:42–47. All they did was teach the Word, pray, have fellowship with one another and share what they had. It was very simple. In community they met locally to carry out the ordinary means of grace. This is what we have been called to do as well in the poorest communities of our world. It's not one plan for the rich suburbs and another plan for the projects. The same thing that happened in Jerusalem 2,000 years ago should be happening everywhere.

Here's the thing: God is glorious. His purposes are glorious. His church is an extension of his glory because it's part of his glorious plan. The poor, like everyone else, therefore need the local church. It brings the greatest glory to God when the means to care for the poor are his means. If he has ordained the local church as the primary place this is to happen, then surely the planting and revitalising of churches in the poorest areas brings glory to God. At the end of the day, the church is Christ's glorious bride and we should be excited to see the establishment of the church in poorer communities.

The church shows God's wisdom

Second, the church shows forth the manifold wisdom of God. Ephesians 3:10 says, 'through the church, the manifold wisdom of God should be made known to the rulers and authorities in the heavenly realms.' In God's magnificent plan of salvation, he has chosen the church to show off his manifold wisdom to the rulers and authorities in the heavenly places. The gospel of Jesus Christ saves people from all sorts of backgrounds and brings them together to worship the same God. The gospel is the great equaliser because it declares that all have fallen short of the glory of God and need grace. The church is the place where we see the gospel made visible.

And it's interesting the word Paul uses in verse 10. He uses the word 'manifold' – the manifold wisdom of God. The word manifold in the text means varied. Think about Joseph and the technicoloured dream coat. The coat was made up of all sorts of different colours. Or think of the endless colours of flowers in spring and summer time. There are yellows, reds, pinks, blues, oranges, greens – all sorts of different shades. It's almost too much to take in when you see all the colours side by side. It's beautiful. It's varied. Or think about a patchwork quilt where different shades of cloth are sewed together. Well, that's the sense of the meaning behind that word manifold here. The church shows the varied wisdom of God.

Specifically, in the book of Ephesians, the manifold wisdom is the fact that Christ is calling both Jew and Gentile to himself. Christ's death has broken down the walls of hostility. In other words, the church was to be made up of all backgrounds. Every different social status. The church is a place where Jew and Gentile, male and female, rich and poor, slave and free, come together to worship God. Therefore, the church brings most glory to God when it is manifold. It should be like an intricate embroidered pattern on a quilt.

However, if it is only made up of one set of people it's not multi-varied. If a certain set of people don't feel welcome in a place, then it is not showing the manifold wisdom of God. If the church is simply full of people who have been university-educated, have big houses, live in certain areas, send their kids to certain schools and hang out with the same people, then it's not manifold. Or if it's just a meeting of people who have all been addicted in a recovery centre and are hanging out with each other, then it's not manifold. The manifold wisdom of God is shown in the diversity that makes up the local church.

Remember God loves the poor. He is the Father of the widow, orphan and the oppressed (Deut. 10:18; Jas. 1:27). If a church is simply made up of the 'haves' then it's not fully displaying God's glory. It's like a patchwork quilt with only one colour. But the church should be the patchwork of different social backgrounds all worshipping the one true God. This brings glory to God.

I grew up with two parents, nice home, Christian family, private school and a university education. Sam (pastoral assistant at Niddrie Community Church) is from a single parent household, with no Christian presence, he dropped out of school and was involved with gangs. We couldn't be any more different. However, doesn't it show the grace of God and the glory of God when he calls two people from different backgrounds out of darkness and into his light and puts them in a church together to worship him and be friends and family in Christ? That is the beauty of the local church.

The church is the place for evangelism

Third, the local church gives a solid, consistent thrust for evangelistic efforts. We see this all throughout the New Testament. Paul went into areas to share the gospel and then he established churches. This was his normal pattern of ministry. It should be ours too.

Healthy local churches keep the spiritual lives of the poor front and centre. Other ministries that focus on alleviating hunger or poverty or supporting children at risk are amazing ministries, but they are a side show to the main thing – which is the salvation of souls. Of course, the healthy church keeps the soul central without neglecting the body. Jesus always cared for body, mind and soul and so should we. John Piper once said as Christians we care about all suffering, but especially eternal suffering. And the greatest way we can care for the most vulnerable is to introduce them to the person who cares most about them: the Lord Jesus Christ and the life that is found in his name.

Here is the thing: the local church offers the best platform for people to hear the gospel. It's when people move into a community, live among its people and seek to share the gospel in word and deed. Why? Because people from schemes and poorer communities aren't dropping into a church in centre of town. Many of our people won't go out of the one-mile radius called home. Unless a church is established, they are not hearing the good news of the gospel. The repeated phrase I hear from people in the schemes is that the church is for posh people. They need to see that it's not just for posh people in town but for people in the schemes as well.

Evangelism also flows out of relationship. It flows from a loving community. How can the poorest see the love of Christ if churches only gather in rich places? If they are going to see the love of Christ, there needs to be a local church meeting to be present!

The key here as is the same anywhere is this: relationship. When you have a mercy ministry it's very difficult to establish a relationship. It's often drive by. However, establishing a healthy local church in an area means that you are coming alongside people over a long period of time. Relationships take time to form. People are often suspicious. They often don't come to you until they hit crisis. We need to be there to share the hope of the gospel in their time of need.

Most of our evangelistic conversations happen in everyday life. Most of the people we've seen converted come from everyday ministries on the ground. They have come through a recovery Bible study group or the cafe or our football team or a friend inviting them to church or youth work. It's taken time and effort to win souls for Christ.

Church provides family to the glory of God

Four, church provides family to the glory of God. The Lord has provided the church so that when a person comes to Christ, they have a genuine spiritual family to come into. This is vital. Those from poorer communities often have broken homes. They have fatherless homes, absent parents, addicted brothers, chaos. It's family but it's difficult. The church should be the place that provides spiritual fathers, mothers, aunties, uncles, brothers and sisters. This brings glory to God.

This is key: local church is family, not handouts. If I provide a service for someone then it creates a them-and-us situation. The relationship changes when we are family serving together. When we are family, we are equal – different roles and functions but everyone is equally part of the family.

A healthy local church is one where people get saved and become part of the family of God. It's not 'Here is a handout and get lost.' It's 'Here is some food, come and be part of something. Come and belong. Come and settle. Come and be loved.'

Remember that Jesus didn't just give out some fish and bread and say, 'On your way.' He said, 'Come and follow me.' He said, 'Come and eat bread that will satisfy. Come and be part of my kingdom.' That is what the church offers. That brings glory to God.

In *Church in Hard Places*, Mez writes this:

> Nick Saul, who worked with food banks across Canada, criticised food banks for being about 'privileged people helping the underprivileged, perpetuating an us-and-them atmosphere.'
>
> Saul believes that traditional food banks don't really help the needy. The food they provide is often poor quality, and the process does nothing to help clients' dignity or self-esteem, get them a job, help them out of poverty or improve their health and well-being. People's immediate hunger is satisfied, but that doesn't last long. Here is his haunting commentary

on most food bank initiatives: 'The only person who is not benefiting is the person who this was set up to help. Most people who must visit food banks say it is a slow, painful death of the soul.'

And if we are honest, most mercy ministries do not accomplish much beyond making the people who run it feel good about themselves. Most church mercy ministries are run by middle class people who love Jesus, and often these people are motivated by a mixture of godly intentions and misplaced guilt. Instead of helping people, too many mercy ministries are content to do things that merely appear to help people. The result is a programme that makes people dependent on handouts and help from the people who are 'above' them on the social ladder. There is not actually much enduring fruit coming from these ministries, but no one wants to cut them lest they seem unconcerned about the poor.'[1]

This is what we must avoid in all aspects of ministry, not simply food banks. This is not a them-and-us thing. This is a come-and-follow-Jesus-and-we-will-serve-together thing. This is a come-and-join-a-family. It's easy to give out food – it's far harder but more glorious to build a relationship with a person. It's easy to see people once a week for an hour – it's far harder but more glorious to serve side by side for the sake of the gospel. The church allows this to happen. It's not poor and rich but sinners saved by grace. It's not them and us but we are all the body seeking to be the local church.

---

1 McConnell, *Church in Hard Places*.

Church provides boundaries and accountability

Five, church provides boundaries and accountability. Every person needs boundaries. We see that with children. The happiest children are those that know the boundaries and have learned to live within them. If someone is given what they want all the time, then they become spoilt. If someone is given no rules at all and no accountability, then chaos ensues. We see both in our communities.

The glory of God is protected and God's people too when there are boundaries for all to live within and consequences when those boundaries are broken. This is what biblical membership, accountability and church discipline provides. This is something that the church can offer that para-church organisations cannot. The boundaries help a person to grow. They help both the person who has been spoilt, and the person who had no rules, to change to develop godly character. It also protects the glory of God when a person who claims to be a Christian is simply 'at it' because they can be challenged and removed from membership.

Church gives long term care including discipleship and training

Six, the church gives long-term care including discipleship and training. The healthy church that is established will have an effect through the generations. The healthy church will offer long-term support to the community. The aim of the church is to glorify God, preach the gospel and make disciples. When people are converted and discipled, they then go on to preach the gospel and make disciples. This brings a longevity to the work. Communities and people need long-term care not short-term fixes. The local church offers that to the glory of God. This happens as healthy local churches offer a context in which young converts and believers can grow in discipleship and community together.

Mez writes:

> When the Lord blesses our efforts and we see evangelistic fruit from our efforts, we must be ready to disciple the new converts and help them to engage and minister fully in the life of the congregation. But if we have started a mercy ministry with no plan beyond the crisis intervention stage, we will never get beyond the very first stages of discipleship with a needy person. And so, churches need to think through the long-term ramifications of their ministry to the poor. We must think about what we are going to do with somebody who comes to faith through a mercy ministry. What is the discipleship strategy? Who will care for them? Who will hold them accountable? How will we move them forward in their walk with Jesus? How will we prepare them for whatever works of service God has called them to once he has saved them? How will we identify and train the former drug dealers and homeless people and sexual predators that the Lord is calling into full-time ministry?[2]

---

2 McConnell, *Church in Hard Places*.

Conclusion

The Lord Jesus loves the church. The Lord Jesus also loves the poor. So, isn't it glorifying to God when we plant gospel churches in the poorest communities of our world?

At 20Schemes we are not looking to build churches that only have a heart for the poor but seeking to build a church of God-worshippers in the heart of a deprived scheme. Big difference. As Mez McConnell has written on the Niddrie blog:

> A God glorifying, Bible believing, gospel preaching, actively discipling, healthy, local church living in Christian community, serving, and loving one another is going to make an impact in a housing scheme. It is what we desperately need. Even a small, tightly knit band of brothers and sisters is going to affect cultural and community renewal.[3]

Acts 2:42–47 tells us what church looked like for the early Christians believers:

> They devoted themselves to the apostles' teaching and to fellowship, to the breaking of bread and to prayer. Everyone was filled with awe at the many wonders and signs performed by the apostles. All the believers were together and had everything in common. They sold property and possessions to give to anyone who had need. Every day they continued to meet together in the temple courts. They broke bread in their

---

3 Mez McConnell, 'The Role of the Local Church Within Deprived Communities (2)', Niddrie Community Church blog, https://niddrie.org/the-role-of-the-local-church-within-deprived-communities-2/. Accessed 22/05/2023.

homes and ate together with glad and sincere hearts, praising God and enjoying the favour of all the people. And the Lord added to their number daily those who were being saved.

Imagine if we had small gatherings like that in schemes across Scotland. What difference would that make!

Three snap shots

I first came to a service at Niddrie in 2008. There was a lady bashing out some *Mission Praise* tunes on an old keyboard. There were no children to be seen. People were nice but the church didn't seem to be having any impact in the community. It didn't feel like there was a lot of life.

Fast forward to Niddrie in 2014. That's when we baptised our first convert and we took on our first indigenous trainee. We had a staff team of two ex-addicts, two local ladies and four people who were from other council estates. It was manic.

And Niddrie 2022. Ten years of 20Schemes and Niddrie is flourishing. Churches are being planted. We've recently had two baptisms of relatives of people who have been converted. We have a multi-socio-economic church membership. We have couples fostering kids, single mothers, ex-addicts, social workers, accountants and NHS workers. All glory be to God.

7. Membership:
How church membership killed our church plant and why I'm glad it did

Pete Stewart
Pastor, Hope Community Church, Barlanark;
West of Scotland Hub Director

It was the best of times, it was the worst of times, it was the age of wisdom, it was the age of foolishness. It was Glasgow, Scotland, in the late 2000s. Let me tell you a (short) tale of two churches ...

Both churches were led by church planters not from the context, but with many people who were. Both had the generous support of American churches to get them off the ground. Both had the Bible, the gospel and the people of Glasgow at their heart. Both had gathered an eclectic group of Christians as part of their plant teams. But the approach of each church towards church membership was poles apart.

Church 'A' was led by a gifted, engaging charismatic leader. He was a visionary. He was a preacher. He could gather a crowd. And his vision of a church family who loved Jesus, loved each other, and loved the city was captivating for many Christians stuck in a rut of old-fashioned religion and the well-worn paths of ministry that seemed far less effective in our postmodern culture. So, Church 'A' quickly grew into a church of diverse people in every sense. They were diverse culturally, theologically, in personality and in gifting – but they were united in their love of Jesus and their commitment to his mission. There was no formal church membership, but there was a loving church family, and God was on the move.

Church 'B' didn't quite have the same level of panache. There were leaders. There were preachers. And there was a vision to engage with the type of communities long forgotten by the mainstream church. So again, people came and people wanted to be involved. People who loved Jesus, people who were growing in love with each other and people who wanted to love and reach the least, the last and the lost. But then it all came crashing down ... Why? Because they implemented formal church membership. In the lead up to the launch, it meant a team of 16 adults reduced to a team of 7 because of differences in theological issues like baptism, eldership and membership, because of an inability to commit to a church covenant that defined what it would mean for them to 'flee from sin' – and because, ultimately, the team didn't want to formally commit to be a church.

I wonder what church you would want to be part of if you had a choice. If I told you only one of these churches is still a church today, which one would you think?

I'm sure you can tell by now, but the church Pete Bell and I planted (Hope Community Church, Barlanark) is Church 'B'. We were meant to launch (or as my friend Nathan would tell me to say 'covenant together') at Easter 2017. But the concept of 'church membership' killed our church plant, and I'm glad it did. For in the remaining months of that year, with the relentless support of 20schemes, the Lord gathered a group that weren't just united on vision but united as a church. We learned a lot in those months about the type of furnace that church unity is formed in, and the type of commitment that 'church membership' is meant to bring. So, in January 2018 we became our own church, and, by the Lord's grace, we have grown (steadily but continually) since then and are now the Hub of 20schemes' church planting operations in the West of Scotland. God has been good, and (at least from my viewpoint) our approach has been vindicated.

Church 'A' launched and grew quickly, but in the two years after that it all fell apart. Unfortunately, the charismatic leader had been hiding disqualifying sin for years, and when he was caught red-handed, the church had to step in and step him out. Yet without the structures of membership, they really struggled to make decisions and find a common direction. The challenges of an eclectic mix of theology became more evident without the big personality linking them together. God was still good, and most of them are now flourishing at other good churches, but Church 'A' is now no more, and the lack of formal church membership was (at least from my viewpoint) a key part of the reason why.

Let me share with you some of the lessons I learned from this whole experience.

Every church has church membership

It has become a cliched twenty-first-century phrase, at least among church planters, to say 'Church is a family not a building' – but I think that is true. But the question I would want to ask in return to many who roll this out is, 'So who then is *in* your church family?' The simple fact is that if you don't have a group of people who are 'in' your church, then you might have a building, or you might even have a service, but you don't have a church.

The word 'church' comes from the Greek *ecclesia* which means (at least in part) 'an assembly or congregation' so a church needs to be able to point to *who* is assembling as that family or *who* makes up that congregation. If it can't do that, then in what sense can it call itself a church? I've been really encouraged by the resurgence of church planting in recent years, but I'm also really concerned that the people leading the planting of these churches do not themselves know what a church is.

In our church we often say, 'The Christian life is the local church life.' As we read the New Testament, we see *nothing* of a

Christian who isn't committed to – and, hence, at least in some sense, a 'member' of a local church.[1]

Acts 2 (a favourite passage for church planters) makes this abundantly clear. Acts 2:41 describes the response to Peter's preaching of the gospel by saying 'so those who accepted his message were baptised, and that day about three thousand people were added to them.' People responded by repentance and faith, shown publicly by baptism and then were added to 'them' – but who are the 'them' they were added to?

We see that in verse 42 that, 'They devoted themselves to the apostles' teaching, to the fellowship, to the breaking of bread, and to prayer.' They were added to the group of people who were committed (devoted) to the preaching of the Word, the fellowship of fellow Christians, taking communion ('breaking of bread') with those fellow Christians, all of which was saturated in prayer. In other words, the 'they' was the first New Testament local church – Hope Community Church Jerusalem, if you will.

Local church membership is also implied throughout the rest of the New Testament:

- By the fact most of the Epistles were addressed to local churches. Who made up those churches? Their 'members'.
- By the fact that elders were put in place to shepherd churches (Acts 14:23) and Christians were called to

---

1 Before you whip out the Eunuch from Acts 8 then surely, we must take from that passage that he was sent back to his own context to share the gospel and so plant a local church.

submit to their elders (Heb. 13:17). Who were the elders to shepherd? Every Christian near them? No! Those who had committed to submit to them as elders, in other words, their church members.

- By the fact that the local church (the *ecclesia*) in Matthew 18 was made the final court of appeal for disputes. Who were people to appeal to if the church 'members' were not known?

This issue often gets muddled when people talk about the 'universal church' and the 'local church' as two completely distinct things. But, according to the New Testament, when you zoom in to the 'universal church' map, you should find all the individual members gathered in their own 'local churches'.

Again, we often say, church membership is voluntary – in the sense that you get to choose what church of people you unite to and so what elders you submit to – but it's compulsory in the sense that if you want to follow Jesus the way Jesus calls you to follow Jesus ... you need to do that as part of a local church.

But much more than that, church membership is a blessing. God didn't save us to be islands. We're not meant to battle the devil, the world and our flesh on our own. We get to do that with brothers and sisters (and fathers and mothers) in local churches. It is so heart-breaking to hear many stories in recent years of people who haven't known 'church membership' to be a joy. But if we do it the way the Bible calls us to, it's meant to be for our good. And it's for the good of those we are trying to reach. And ultimately, it's for the glory of God. Every church, if it is a church, has church membership.

Clarity brings unity in church membership

If 'Every church has church membership' then it seems to me, you can do it one of two ways. You can do it the way of Church 'A', organically, without the barriers of formalism, working to cultivate the life of a family. Or you can do it the way of Church 'B' (our church), formally and clearly, believing that it's clarity that brings unity to the family.

When we first started out the church planting journey, we tried to have a wide-open door and gather anyone who loved Jesus and wanted to love the lost in our community. But the more we got into teaching the Bible, the more we realised a lack of clarity on key (albeit non-gospel) issues was having the opposite effect of what we were hoping for. People didn't know what we thought, people didn't know what they were actually committing to, people didn't know what we meant by church and so people didn't know what type of church we were trying to be. So instead of being a committed church 'family', we were far more like a group of people 'dating' and not sure where we were heading.

The more we reflected on passages like 1 Corinthians 12, the more convinced we were that to become a living church 'body' (as Paul calls it in that passage), we needed to have clarity of who the 'members' were. (Incidentally, 'members' is Paul's word not ours. I'm flummoxed when people say church membership isn't in the Bible. I mean, it literally is!) We also needed to have clarity on what each 'member' did. From this we developed several structures that we hoped would help guide and direct the continued organic growth of the church – the same way a trellis might support and direct the growth of a vine.

Some of the structures we found most helpful were things like:

- A clear set of statements for 'What we believe' (what all our members believe about Jesus), 'What we teach' (what all our elders will teach on certain 'non-gospel' issues that may prove challenging to some) and 'How we will live' (our 'church covenant', a collection of Bible verses that call us to live in this way together)
- A clear membership process every member would go through
- A clear commitment that only members would serve in the church (because why would we let someone represent the church who wasn't willing to commit to the church?)
- A clear eldership process for the identifying, training and calling of future church elders
- A clear understanding that being a member of this church means living your life alongside the other members of this church and so being each other's 'family'.

Many would think these processes would zap the life out of a church family, but we have honestly found that they have brought life. People often comment on how much our church feels like family. Many have joined our church because they have found a sense of shared community and life here that they struggled to find anywhere else. And I always tell them it's the clarity we aim to provide that brings this unity we all enjoy.

You could do church membership in the way of Church 'A', and it will probably work for a while certainly when everything is going well. But soon the storms will come ... and when they do, you need clear foundations to keep the church together. The way of Church 'B' might well push against the individualistic and informal tendencies of our twenty-first-century culture, but it provides a lasting sense of the community and life that our twenty-first-century culture longs for. Clarity brings unity in church membership.

Church membership helps us fulfil the Great Commission

A fellow pastor once told me, 'The church isn't God's primary mission strategy, it's God's exclusive mission strategy.' I find that helpful (because it's true!) yet in the poorest communities of our land it's something we often seem to forget. In the last 50 years it seems like 'church planting' has largely been 'church splitting', and even then, it's been in the more middle-class or affluent communities of our cities. In many ways, our poorest communities have been left behind. But even in recent years, when there has been a resurgence of Christians seeking to minister in our poorest communities, ministry to the poor has often been done 'apart from' local churches. There has been an influx of individual Christians or para-church agencies seeking to redress the balance, many (though indeed not all) of these with a good gospel emphasis. But, if the Christian life *is* the local church life and if we are not seeking to see the poorest of our society brought into and then thrive as part of local churches, then what *are* we doing?

I think it's no coincidence that this has happened while church culture at large has taken a step back from the idea of 'formal' (or clear) church membership. But I also think that's a big mistake. For what the people of our poorest communities need most is to be united to Christ and then united to his body as part of the local church. I firmly believe you cannot love the poor, as Jesus loves them, and then not love and so work towards the planting and revitalising of local churches in the poorest areas. Our poorest communities need local churches that take seriously the commitment of church membership.

What difference does church membership make?

Church membership helps us making disciples not converts because it gives new disciples a new family to belong to. If following Jesus means (as it does for many in our context) leaving behind a peer group who were family, then we need to be a new family that will help them now flee sin and run to Jesus. Church membership helps make that happen.

It removes the barriers of culture and class. If all we have are projects run by (well-meaning) outsiders reaching needy insiders, then we are going to have groups full of internal and external barriers – not a united loving family. But if we have churches built on the gospel of Jesus and living that out through the commitment of church membership then we will have the type of unity we see in Ephesians 2. We'll have a loving family where the distinctions of rich or poor, young or old, male or female are part of our diversity, but not part of our problem.

It stops us from being patronising and helps us all grow to be more like Christ. If we are all united together through the structures of church membership, then we are all committed to help *each other* grow to be more like Jesus. It means we *all* have a role to play, and we *all* have a voice in how this should be done. It no longer separates the place where we *serve* Jesus from the place where we *grow* in Jesus. Driving in from a 'nice' area to serve in a poorer area and then driving home again makes no sense. It is the opposite of what we are called to do and be. We may be different from each other but we are all sinners – and growing to be more like Jesus happens for us all when we live in a local church community *together*.

Finally, church membership brings most glory to Christ. Jesus only promised to build one body of people, his 'church'. If the universal church is seen visibly in local churches, then, when we grow local churches of his people in all communities of his world, he is most glorified because it is then that his design is most clear and his name is most known. There are many reasons the concept of 'church membership' is a good thing, despite what modern culture tells us, but the glory of Christ surely must be number one.

Conclusion

No matter where we come from in regard to our view of church membership, I'm sure we can all agree that the vibrancy and life that was so clear at the start of Church 'A' is the type of church family we are made for and the type of church family we are each longing for. But I hope this has at least made you think about how we should best get there. Through my study of God's word, conversations with other Christians from many other contexts and experience as one of the pastors of Church 'B', I really believe that (although) 'church membership killed our church plant ... I'm glad it did!' For now, out the other side of it, we have a united church of members who love Jesus, love each other and have committed to love the lost through the best of times and through the worst of times until Jesus calls us home.

8. Doctrine:
Atonement and election – the gift of salvation applied to the graft of Ministry

Andy Prime
Gracemount Community Church, Edinburgh

Ministry in the schemes of Scotland is hard. The pastors and planters in 20schemes meet up monthly to pray for each other and the lads always come weary and heavy-laden. The need is overwhelming. The investment needed is huge. The discouragements are relentless. At times it's easy to lose sight of the goodness of the God who called us here. At times it's easy to be so busy trying to offer the gospel to others that we stop resting in that gospel ourselves.

That weariness comes from the fact that we're often ministering to people who have deep wounds. We often say that 'the deepest wounds need the deepest doctrine.' That's why central to our ministry in the schemes is the articulation and application of the gospel in all its infinite richness and depth. That's what the people we're ministering to need most. But it's also what *we* need most. What will keep us going when we're tempted to give up? What will refresh us when we're weary with sorrow? What will keep us faithful to Jesus until the very end? What will fill us up so that we've got something to overflow into the lives of others? Only the infinite richness and depth of the gospel.

And so, the aim of this chapter is to take two doctrines of the Christian faith, to define them briefly, and then attempt to apply them deeply.

- **Atonement:** The work of Jesus – in his life and death – to cleanse us from our sin and satisfy the wrath of God, to restore our relationship with God.
- **Election:** The work of God – before the creation of the world – to choose some people to be saved, not based on anything they will do, but based on what Jesus will do for them.

Atonement

Atonement centres me on what's important

When I'm confronted with a million problems, atonement centres me on what's most important. For some of us, this might just be what we wake up to most mornings: a million problems. The cat's brought home a dead mouse. Bills are due. Internet's been cut off. Kids are at war. Family dramas escalating. Health's declining. Neighbours are noisy. And someone finished the

Doctrine

Coco Pops! But if you've trusted in the work of Jesus to atone for your sins – to cleanse you and satisfy God – then although your relationship with everything in the world is panicked, your relationship with the Judge of all the world is peace. Atonement means, even if my circumstances are wild, I can still say, 'It is well with my soul.'

But for some of us we're not just confronted with that in our own homes, but we're confronted with more of it in ministry. Last week I stood in a flat that I'd been told was possessed by demons, with two massively anxious parents, some terrified kids, a screaming baby, and a bulldog trying to hump my leg and lick my face! In moments like that there's a million things confronting you, and a million things you feel compelled to do to help. You could end up trying to multi-task the roles of super-nanny, social worker, food bank volunteer, rehab-worker, exorcist and delivery driver.

But where does the atonement centre me? I could invest my energy in helping them have the most well-behaved kids, with cupboards rammed with food, parents with months of sobriety and a flat that looked like a show-home. But unless they've had their sins cleansed and the wrath of God satisfied by Jesus, then all I've done is resurfaced the road to hell so that it's slightly less bumpy. That may be more comfortable for them and may be more culturally acceptable to majority Christianity, but they are no more acceptable before God. As a Christian, a friend and a pastor, the atonement centres me on the unique thing I have to offer people that no other service in our community is offering. Don't lose your centre.

Atonement comforts me that I've been washed clean

Secondly, when I'm crippled by the guilt of my past, atonement comforts me that I've been washed clean. I don't know about you, but the most crippling thing to me is not being confronted by other people's problems. It's being confronted again and again by my own sin. I have an unbelievable capacity to forget important things: our anniversary, Bible verses, my son's name, to reply to emails. But I find it unbelievably impossible to shift the memories of my past shame. And it cripples me. The evil one can use it to make me hate my identity, wonder if God still loves me and question my fitness for ministry.

How does the atonement comfort me when I'm crippled with doubt and fear? Let's jump to Leviticus, because if the centre of atonement in the New Testament is the cross, then the centre of atonement in the Old Testament is Leviticus 16. Here we discover The Day of Atonement's dramatized by two goats. The first one is slaughtered in the presence of God. It shows *how* atonement is achieved. For my sin to be cleansed, it needs to be put onto another. For God's wrath to be diverted from me, it needs to be diverted onto another. The goat's blood is shed, and its life is sacrificed, so that mine can be spared.

But then comes the second goat. It's not showing *how* atonement is achieved – but applying *what* atonement has achieved. And it's not slaughtered, it's sent away. Driven into the wilderness, never to return. When I'm crippled by the guilt of my past that keeps coming back, I need to remember the goat that never came back. It took my sin as far as east is from west. That's the glory of the gospel in the goat that's gone.

In Isaiah 43:25 and 38:17, we discover that the forgivingness which takes place *after the atonement* is so perfect that it can be called *a blotting out* or *a casting behind one's back*. In Micah 7:19, it is a picture of casting our sins into the depths of the sea. We need to drink deeply from the well of this truth. Therefore, when I use the word 'comfort', I'm not meaning soft, padded toilet-roll-type comfort. I'm talking biblical, courage-giving, spine-strengthening comfort.

Atonement reminds me that God sees me as he sees Jesus

Thirdly, when it seems like my sin pollutes everything I do, the doctrine of atonement reminds me that God sees me as he sees Jesus. One moment we're speaking about the gospel in all its purity. The next moment what's coming out our mouths is just pure pollution. Or we have a few days where we're right on it in our Christian walk and involved in ministry. And then the next day we're right back in a relapse like a dog to its vomit.

For me it can be in the moment when I'm teaching or preaching from the Bible, and my impure motives for approval or applause muddy and contaminate the whole thing. Sometimes I am overwhelmed by my own sinful depravity. But that's not always a good or healthy thing. There's nothing spiritually healthy about wallowing in my filthy rags. It might sound spiritual, but it's not if all I am communicating is how disappointed and frustrated God is with me. Maybe that's what we inherited from our sin-polluted experience of worldly fathers, but that's not what the atonement should say to us. It tells us that:

Our sins have been cleansed. Our Heavenly Father's wrath has been satisfied. God doesn't see us as filthy rags. God sees us as he sees his beloved Son. We're running into the realm of justification. But that's alright. Atonement means it's not just that Jesus takes my sin. It's that he gives me his righteousness.

Think that through. Let me repeat it. God does not just take away our sins in Jesus. He also gives us his righteousness. In other words, when God looks upon the Christian, he looks upon us with *the same love and acceptance as he does his sinless Son.*

The artwork my son brings home from nursery is poor by anyone's standards. But I love them because I love him. Our efforts in following Jesus may be comparable to my son's artwork, but he loves them because in Christ he loves us. He loves you. He's for you. And he loves to bless and reward his children.

Atonement ends with one-ness with God

When it begins to feel like I'm all on my own, atonement ends with one-ness with God. Becoming a Christian in a scheme can be very isolating. We may have to walk away from a whole family or peer-group. It might mean a life of singleness and celibacy. It might mean a whole host of difficulties. But where we've touched on some of the benefits of the atonement, this takes us to the ultimate purpose of the atonement.

In 1 Peter 3:18. We read, 'For Christ also suffered once for sins, the righteous for the unrighteous, to bring you to God.'

Here it is again.

- 'For Christ also suffered once for sins': that's the *means* of the atonement, how it was achieved
- 'the righteous for the unrighteous' – there's the *mechanism* of the atonement (Jesus substituting himself for us)
- 'to bring you to God' – the *purpose* of the atonement. Why did he do it? To bring you to God.

We need to digest this. The ultimate purpose of what Christ has done is *not* about removing your sin. The ultimate purpose of what Christ has done is *not* about making you righteous. They are both vital points on the journey but they're not the destination. The atonement is not just God doing something *to you*. It's about God doing something to you *so that* you can be *brought to him*. The purpose of the atonement is the massive purpose of God's promise in Jeremiah 30:22: 'You will be my people, and I will be your God.'

Even when we feel most alone, we're not alone. Atonement is not just about us escaping hell. It's about us embracing the Father. It's about union with Christ. It's about the indwelling of the Spirit. The answer to our loneliness is not more friends, but more closeness to God. Before it's about community with other people, it's about communion with God.

Atonement clarifies the grace of God

When I'm confused by election, atonement clarifies the grace of God. The purpose of this point is to help our transition to the doctrine of election. Many Christians struggle with, rather than rest in, this doctrine. Many more see the doctrine in Scripture but struggle to verbalise it for their own life. Some struggle with the thought of God choosing some and not others, particularly when unbelieving loved ones die. But here's how the atonement helps give us clarity when we're confused.

When we see God through Christ cleanse us from the sin we've committed, remove from us the wrath we've earned, rescue us from the hell we deserved, it doesn't leave us questioning *why he only saves some*, rather it leaves us amazed that *he'd even save one*.

Our sin left us so dead that salvation must be from God from start to finish, so undeserving that salvation must be by grace from start to finish.

Therefore, the atonement clarifies for us that from God's choice in eternity, to Christ's work at Calvary, to the response in us personally, is grace from top to bottom, start to finish, and all the way through to the end of life.

Election

And now on to applying election to the graft of ministry.

Let's just remind ourselves of our definition: election is the work of God – before the creation of the world – to choose

Doctrine

some people to be saved, not based on anything they will do, but based on what Jesus will do for them.

Election reminds me that nothing but God's grace saved me

When I drift into my self-righteous-saviour-complex, election drives me back to acknowledge that nothing but God's free grace saved me. I may be on my own here. But there's some hugely unhelpful places my heart can take me. The longer I go on as a Christian, and the further away I am from the old me, the easier it is to forget what God saved me from. The more I'm confronted by other people's problems, the easier it is to be proud of where my life has got to. The more I invest in someone only for them to then turn away or throw it back in my face, there's a tendency for my heart to think the difference between them and me is not God's grace, but my work.

Or when someone becomes a Christian, it's easy to think it was all down to me, and then to over-invest in discipleship because I presume their new life can't survive without my life-support. And before I know it, I am swanning about the scheme not just wearing the long flowing robes of a Pharisee, but the flowing cape of a super-hero. But here's where election drives me to when I'm drifting there. If it wasn't for the work of God the Father before creation choosing me, and if it wasn't for the work of the Spirit before conversion re-creating me, then I'm still dead in my sins too.

We're drifting from election to regeneration, but that's cool. Because without God's work electing me and the Spirit's work regenerating me, the Son's work in the atonement would simply be a beautiful song I didn't have the ears to hear; a perfect achievement that I didn't have the ability to apply; a wonderful meal I didn't have the taste buds to appreciate; good news that I was too dead to realise was news at all.

I'm undeservingly chosen by God, renewed by the Spirit and righteous only in Christ. I think this is most profoundly and simply communicated by Paul in a little phrase at the start of 1 Corinthians 1:30, 'It is because of him that you are in Christ Jesus'. Why am I a Christian? How am I 'in Christ'? It is because of Him.

> O how the grace of God
> amazes me!
> It loosed me from my bonds
> and set me free!
> What made it happen so?
> His own will, this much I know,
> Set me, as now I show,
> at liberty.

> My God has chosen me,
> Though one of nought,
> To sit beside my King
> in heaven's court.
> Hear what my Lord has done,
> O, the love that made Him run
> To meet His erring son!
> This has God wrought.

> Not for my righteousness,
> for I have none,
> But for His mercy's sake,
> Jesus, God's Son,
> Suffered on Calvary's tree;
> Crucified with thieves was He;
> Great was His grace to me,
> His wayward one.[1]

Election reminds me to take off my robes and my cape. As 1 Corinthians 1:31 says, 'Let the one who boasts boast in the Lord.'

Election reminds me not to write people off

When I'm tempted to write people off as unsavable, election reminds me of whose names are written in the book of life. Sometimes I'm tempted to unfairly judge this under the Christian cloak of 'discernment'. Because I've got limited time, energy and ability, I'll be selective about who's worth 'investing' in. I doubt people for any number of reasons. Some people look too far gone to be truly helped. Some families seem hopelessly lost in abuse and addictions. Some people look like they would be too much work to teach and disciple. Some people appear like they would be impervious to the preaching of the gospel. I look at many people in the scheme and Jeremiah 4:22 resonates within me. 'They are skilled in doing evil; they know not how to do good.'

---

1 Emanuel T. Sibomana, trans. Rosemary Guillebaud, 'O How the Grace of God', 1946, copyright: Church Mission Society.

They know not how to do good. That's just where some people are at. That's what we face as we reach out in our communities. We don't just *do* evil. We don't just *love* evil. We're *skilled* at it. It's not just that we don't do what's good. It's that we don't even know how to do good. How does someone get saved out of that? How do we reach people who have been groomed since childhood to run drugs, and to ignore the law? How can they ever be saved?

But what does election remind me? That God's grace is *powerful*. That God's grace is *irresistible*. When I'm tempted to doubt God's saving power, I need to remember the type of people whose names God has written in *his* book of life. If it had been left to me, I would have written most, if not all, of them off. Moses and David weren't coming back from murder and adultery. Nebuchadnezzar was too full of himself and too busy building idols to acknowledge God. Rahab, the 'sinful' woman in Luke 7, and the Samaritan woman in John 4, were too covered in shame. Legion was too uncontrollable. Zacchaeus and Matthew were too rich to be needy, and too detested to be accepted. The thief on the cross had run out of time. Prominent women in Acts seemed too prominent in their communities to become prominent in the church. Saul of Tarsus had too much blood on his hands. Crispus, the leader of the synagogue Paul had just been kicked out of in Acts 18, was too engrained in his anti-Jesus culture to come out. Onesimus had burned his bridges too much to ever return.

We could go on and on in the Bible, with name after name. We could go on and on in our churches, with member after

Doctrine

member. We could go on and on with our own stories of God's miraculous intervention. Many of us would have been considered write offs, from an earthly point of view. But each one of us is written into the book of life, from an *election* point of view. God's grace is powerful. His arm is not too short.

Therefore, it's not my job to choose where to cast the net. God just tells me to cast it wide. It's not my job to choose where I sow the seed. God tells me to sow it everywhere. Even on rocky ground.

Election assures me that God knows those who are his

Thirdly, when Christians wander beyond our care, election assures me that God knows those who are his. The chances are that every Christian in every church could name at least one person in their life who is wandering from the Lord. Maybe they are going back to their old life. Despite our efforts, they are not responding to messages. Their attendance at church has dropped to a minimum. They have given up hanging out with other believers. There's the agony of seeing them walk away, compounded with the pain of not being able to do a thing about it. How does election bring assurance to us in these moments?

In 2 Timothy 2:19 we are reminded that, 'The Lord knows those who are his.' In 1 John 2:19 we are told that many *professing* Christians who have walked away from the faith, never, in fact, really belonged to Jesus in the first place. All those he foreknew, predestined, called and justified, he'll glorify, Paul says in Romans 8.

Think of the son who squandered his wealth in wild living in Luke 15:13. He went far away from his father but was brought to his senses in Luke 15:17. We recall the apostle Peter who denied Jesus three times, and yet was the rock upon which Jesus built his church. Then there's the man who's sleeping with his mother-in-law and is handed over to Satan (1 Cor. 5) but is forgiven, comforted and loved when he returns in repentance (2 Cor. 2).

Christians who wander beyond our care in this world are not beyond the care of the Father who elected them before the creation of this world. My assurance is not in their ability to return, or my ability to pursue, but in God's ability to keep. We must hold out the promise of Jesus in John 10:28-29, 'I give them eternal life, and they shall never perish; no one will snatch them out of my hand. My Father, who has given them to me, is greater than all; no one can snatch them out of my Father's hand.'

Election keeps me persevering

When I'm almost at the point of giving up, election is the promise that keeps me persevering. Paul entering Corinth is a significant moment in the book of Acts. We know that he walked in weakness and trembling. He'd been imprisoned in Philippi, ran out by the mob in Thessalonica, chased out of Berea, separated from Silas and Timothy, on his own and sneered at in Athens, and now alone in Corinth. *How was he feeling*? Worse than some of us are right now. And that's saying something!

But for all his weakness and trembling, a lot comes together in Corinth. He partners with Priscilla and Aquila who'll become lifelong partners in ministry. He's reunited with Timothy and Silas who bring him a gift from Macedonia for the suffering saints in Jerusalem. We can imagine the boost Paul feels as he goes from being alone and empty handed to surrounded and supported.

In Corinth Jesus doesn't just give Paul community and cash. He gives himself to Paul – his presence and his promises. We read the following in Acts 18:9-10, 'One night the Lord spoke to Paul in a vision: "Do not be afraid; keep on speaking, do not be silent. For I am with you, and no one is going to attack and harm you, because I have many people in this city."' Because of this vision Paul stayed in Corinth for a further eighteen months, knowing that Jesus was with him, that Jesus was protecting him, and that Jesus had people who would get saved as he spoke.

In the spiritual graveyard of Corinth were dry bones into whom the Spirit would breathe new life, as Paul preached the gospel. Paul didn't know who these people were. He didn't know those whom God had chosen in eternity. He didn't know which sermon would be the one to convict sinners. All he had was the promise that God would be with him as he faithfully preached.

Election was God's promise to Paul, and it is his promise to us. God's sovereign electing power is the promise of our success in this generation and beyond. Not success as the world defines it, but success as God predestined it. Our task is not to raise the dead. Our task is to keep preaching in the graveyard God has assigned to us.

Election fills me with reasons for praise

Lastly, when life is full of problems, election fills me with reasons for praise. Let's end by turning to the book of Ephesians. Ephesus was a place Paul knew well, with elders he loved deeply. It was a city that was fascinated by dark arts and the occult. Paul had been caught up in a riot there when he'd preached Jesus. He'd warned the church leaders that savage wolves would come in after he'd left to try to destroy the church.

His letter reveals serious division in the church between people groups. It reveals Paul's awareness of Satan's schemes, and the spiritual warfare that will make life for Christians a constant struggle. As he sits down to write this letter his mind would have been full of all the problems they'd be facing. But just listen to his tone as he starts the letter. He starts the letter the way we, as Christians, ought to start and end each day. The doctrine of God's sovereign election gives us reason for *unrestrained praise* even when life and ministry give us unending reasons to be discouraged.

> Praise be to the God and Father of our Lord Jesus Christ, who has blessed us in the heavenly realms with every spiritual blessing in Christ. For he chose us in him before the creation of the world to be holy and blameless in his sight. In love he predestined us for adoption to sonship through Jesus Christ,

in accordance with his pleasure and will – to the praise of his glorious grace, which he has freely given us in the One he loves (Eph. 1:3–6).

Sermons From The Schemes

9. Dealing with discipline

Mez McConnell
Pastor of Niddrie Community Church, Edinburgh, and Director of 20schemes

Most of the principles I have outlined here are from two books – *God Redeeming His Bride* by Robert Cheong and *Church Discipline* by Jonathan Leeman – and then contextualised for scheme ministry.[1]

Hebrews 12:5-11 says this:

> And have you forgotten the exhortation that addresses you as sons? 'My son, do not regard lightly the discipline of the Lord, nor be weary when reproved by him. For the Lord disciplines the one he loves, and chastises every son whom he receives.' It is for discipline that you have to endure. God is treating you as sons. For what son is there whom his father does not discipline? If you are left without discipline, in which all have

---

1 Robert K. Cheong, *God Redeeming His Bride: A Handbook for Church Discipline,* Christian Focus, 2012 and Jonathan Leeman, *Understanding Church Discipline,* Broadman & Holman, 2016.

> participated, then you are illegitimate children and not sons. Besides this, we have had earthly fathers who disciplined us, and we respected them. Shall we not much more be subject to the Father of spirits and live? For they disciplined us for a short time as it seemed best to them, but he disciplines us for our good, that we may share his holiness. For the moment all discipline seems painful rather than pleasant, but later it yields the peaceful fruit of righteousness to those who have been trained by it.

When we think of church planting and revitalisation, we almost never connect it to church discipline. It is such a neglected teaching, and yet it is vitally important to the health of every church. I remember years ago a church planting friend of mine was arguing with me about church discipline. He just didn't see the need for it. He thought it was a bit heavy-handed, even cult-like. 'Give it a couple of years of church planting and then get back to me,' I told my friend. 'It may seem like a weird topic to discuss now but wait till you get some sinners saved.'

The modern church planter invariably has a great business plan and missionary strategy when they start out. They map out their vision for the next three to five years. The problem is that I have yet to read any plan or strategy that lays out how these men will handle conflict and sin once people begin to be saved.

How will we deal with those who fall into serious sin? What happens when the person who professes faith is sleeping around? What do we do when the person who professes faith is part of a gang and still smokes drugs at night? What authority do we have to challenge them? How do we tell the local, unbelieving community that this person is no longer living up to their profession of faith? How do we protect the purity of the gospel?

Every church leader needs to think about these kinds of questions. In over twenty years of ministry, I have become more and more convinced that church planters, pastors and church revitalisers need to have thought through these issues long before they engage in any serious ministry in our context.

What is church discipline and why do we need it?

Church discipline ought to be an overflow of our discipleship. It's *formative* in that we teach people how to live as Christians so that they live in line with their profession of faith. And it's *corrective* when someone is wandering away from the gospel.

Church discipline is a vital ministry for two big reasons. First, it's required to protect the glory of Christ. We are new creations as Christians, but we still battle with the old man. Church discipline is *correcting sin for the purpose of ensuring that church members are representing Jesus rightly*. It's about calling all Christians to be what they say they are. Every believer has a duty to *protect* the witness of the church and the purity of the gospel of Jesus Christ. This means that when someone is not living in line with their profession of faith, we challenge them so that they do not bring the gospel into disrepute.

This is important in the schemes where we live in such tight communities, where people live on top of each other and where anything that is happening is broadcast on Facebook and other social media. It's not like a gathered church where we can keep things under wraps and hide our little sins. Sin in a scheme is always public and so we must ensure that the community around us knows who's in and who's out.

Secondly, we need church discipline because *it's good for our souls* and *it helps us to grow*. Many professing Christians think that it's unloving to have rules and discipline in the church. They view it as heavy shepherding or as a form of spiritual bullying. But as we read in Hebrews 12, God disciplines those he loves so that they might produce a harvest of righteousness. When we discipline our children, we do that out of love. They need it to grow. The same is true for Christians in the local church. We need to teach our churches that discipline is important for the health of the individual believer and the wider church body. We do not engage in church discipline because we are being harsh, but because we love the Lord Jesus and want to see his people mature in the faith.

Jonathan Leeman writes of four ways that church discipline demonstrates love:

- It shows love for the *individual*, that he or she might be warned and brought to repentance
- It shows love for the *church*, that weaker sheep might be protected
- It shows love for the *watching world*, that it might see Christ's transforming power
- It shows love for *Christ*, that churches might uphold his holy name and obey him.

When should we engage in church discipline?

Let me walk through how we do things at Niddrie Community Church. The fundamentals of church discipline are found in Matthew 18:15-17:

> If your brother sins against you, go and tell him his fault, between you and him alone. If he listens to you, you have gained your brother. But if he does not listen, take one or two others along with you, that every charge may be established by the evidence of two or three witnesses. If he refuses to listen to them, tell it to the church. And if he refuses to listen even to the church, let him be to you as a Gentile and a tax collector.

The first port of call in any church discipline situation is challenging one another *privately*. This should be happening as a matter of course in our discipling relationships within the local body. In fact, 90% of church discipline should be happening between brothers and sisters in Christ on an individual level.

I always make it clear to our members that church discipline is not just for the elders. Most issues wouldn't become 'big' and end up at the elders' feet if we practised Matthew 18 more regularly. We need to be teaching our people the importance of *one anothering*. We need to foster a culture of open discipleship in our churches. We need to give one another permission to challenge any sin in us that might be bringing the gospel, and the witness of the church, into disrepute.

But what happens if that fails? That's when we take the next step laid out in Matthew 18. The issue moves from private to public. We now challenge the sinning brother or sister in the presence of one or two mature witnesses. My advice to the members of my church is that if this becomes necessary, make sure you take along a mature Christian, and not your best friend. Challenge the sin again.

But what happens if that fails? If it still cannot be resolved at this point, then our church elders will become involved. We will discuss the issue, pray about it and then listen to the issues being addressed. After that, we will rebuke and correct anything that needs to be rebuked and corrected.

But what happens if that fails? if there is still no repentance then we will take it to our church members. At Niddrie we operate something called, 'the care list' which is a step prior to removing a person from membership. We do this when a sin has become public and when we as elders have exhausted our counsel. The care list is the elders asking the church to intervene and pray for those people. We will tell the church what is going on and ask them to pray, call, text, email, write to this person and call them to repentance.

But what happens if that fails? If the person is still not repentant then we, as a church body, will remove the person from membership. We treat them as an unbeliever. This means that as a church we cannot affirm the person's profession of faith and, because of this, they are no longer able to take communion. They are excommunicated – removed from the Lord's Table.

From private to public

How do we decide when something is moving from private challenge to public? We only make it public when a sin is: outward, serious and unrepentant. Let's take the example of a lie. Sometimes lies just pop out of our mouths. Maybe we *embellish* a story or conveniently *forget* some detail of a conversation. Perhaps, we feel convicted the moment it leaves our lips and we immediately confess it to God. But what about if a professing Christian is lying consistently and falsely claiming child benefit? It's come up in a conversation and they have been challenged about it. The guilty party tries to justify it, and they see no reason to change their behaviour.

One of these is an everyday sin, quickly confessed and turned away from. The other is an entrenched pattern of sinful behaviour that indicates the person is, consistently, not living in a Christ-honouring way. One is an ongoing struggle between the old man and the new, and the other is just the old man having his cake and eating it! If somebody has been truly born again, then they cannot *settle with their sin*. The Holy Spirit just does not allow it. He provokes and he convicts, and he does it in such a way that it's impossible to even sleep or have any peace until the matter is sorted out and the sinner is pushed to do the right thing whatever the cost.

Therefore, church discipline only becomes public if a church member continues to live in an *openly sinful manner* without any real sign of repentance and change. It becomes public if there is no evidence of Holy Spirit inspired conviction. Feeling guilt or shame is one thing, but it is nothing more than worldly sorrow if it doesn't lead to a turning away from the sin in question. Feeling bad for a short period of time is not a fruit of the Spirit. In the event of a continued pattern of consistent disobedience this would cause the church to question this person's confession of faith. Their life contradicts their profession. At this point we remove their spiritual passport and declare that they are no longer credible representatives of the kingdom of God.

Disciplining messy people in messy churches, in a messy world

This all sounds good in theory, but does it really work in the reality of our sin-stained world? What do we do when a recently converted member gets taken to court for assaulting a neighbour? What do we do when a member struggling with drink, gets drunk, robs a newsagent and jumps a taxi? Would it make a difference in how to proceed if he confessed it first and was now tearily apologising? What do we do when a marriage is breaking down, but the couple persistently lie to us and turn up to church each week saying that everything is fine? What do we do when one of our members struggles with drugs and we suspect that he has gone back to using? The problem is that we don't have cast iron proof, but we are confident that he or she is up to no good. How will we deal with the member who has got a girl in the church pregnant, and they both say they are sorry and want to honour God?

These are real life cases without any simple solutions. Our world is getting messier, not better. Sin is becoming more prevalent, not less. Often, the elders of our church sit with head in hands wondering how to deal with certain situations. Often there are no easy solutions, and it often feels like we must go with the least bad solution. Church discipline is sorted out with great difficulty, pain, prayer, discernment, and even more prayer!

Helpful principles

Bearing all this in mind, let me outline five principles that might be helpful for us as we seek to honour Christ through church discipline in our local churches.

(1) Church discipline needs to take into consideration the circumstances of the individual.

Imagine two church members have gone out over the weekend and scored some heroin. One of them is immediately, and publicly, put on the care list while the other is privately challenged about his behaviour. How is this fair if both have committed the same sin?

This is where background information comes into play. The one dealt with more leniently is a six-week-old Christian who met some of his old friends from the scheme and went back to their flat for a hit. However, he has quickly admitted his sin, taken full responsibility for it and now he says he is repentant. The one whose sin was made immediately public has been claiming to be a Christian for several years. During that time there have been countless incidents like these, as a well as a pattern of lying and manipulation. He has only admitted his guilt after another church member saw him leaving a dealer's house. His posture to spiritual challenge is aggressive denial. Armed with this information, we would deal with these two people very differently.

We must be careful not to expect instant spiritual maturity, especially when dealing with those professing faith out of an addiction background. I expect to see different levels of maturity from a six-week-old Christian and a six-year-old Christian. A six-month-old baby is not eating the same food as a six-year-old child. Their understanding of the world and their place in it is far different. When we are discipling people, we need to ask ourselves:

How long have they been Christians? How much of the Bible do they understand? Do they admit sin? Do they seem grieved over the sin or merely annoyed that you have brought it up? Did they confess the sin or was it uncovered? Do they appear teachable? Are they open to correction? Are they defending or justifying their actions, or are they seeing it for what it is? Are there background factors that make the sin occurring more likely to happen? Were they led into sin by others, or have they led others in sin?

(2) Repentance is key to how quickly we move through church discipline.

We need to ask ourselves the question: Is this person seriously fighting their ongoing sin or not? Jesus is clear in Matthew 18:9, when he says: 'And if your eye causes you to sin, tear it out and throw it away. It is better for you to enter life with one eye than with two eyes to be thrown into the hell of fire.' Repentant people are zealous about moving away from their sin. They are willing to do whatever it takes. End relationships. Hand over their finances. Be publicly accountable. They come to every meeting you set. They turn up and study the Bible. They don't keep putting things off or making excuses.

We need spiritual discernment to distinguish between godly repentance and worldly sorrow. I've had many people in my office crying over what they have done, yet they've not been repentant. One of the other problems we face in our churches is how quickly people pick up religious terminology. They will say all the right things when challenged about their sin. They will say that they have sinned against God. They will say that they want to change. They will say that they love Jesus. But, again, none of these statements is necessarily a sign of repentance.

Repentance means owning your sin, turning away from it and then doing something about it to move forward. Repentance is not feeling sorry for yourself. There is a big difference. Let me give you an example. Bob came to our local church about five years ago. He was battling a heavy cocaine addiction. He also came with several mental health issues. He started off well. He grew in his knowledge of the Bible. He showed initial signs of spiritual growth in his life. He got a job. He had a flat for the first time in years having lived on his streets for a large part of his life. But one night he was caught buying marijuana from a local dealer. He was challenged. He was outwardly repentant. We kept it private because he was a new Christian at this point.

A few months later he bought more marijuana and smoked it. This time two of us challenged him and, again, he was outwardly repentant. He said he wanted to move forward with Jesus. He was in tears. He said he loved Jesus. Again, he was still a new Christian at this point, and so we warned him sternly and kept things private. But, over the next year his behaviour started becoming more chaotic and erratic. A pattern began to develop. He would be clean for a couple of months, then go on a three-to-five-day bender. He would switch his phone off and refuse to answer the door at his flat. But, once the money ran out and the drugs had been used, he returned to the church, tearfully admitting what he had done and promising to never go back.

A few months later and he disappeared off the church's radar. He didn't use his flat anymore. Instead, he slept at fellow drug users' houses. Tragically, at this point we knew he wasn't repentant and so we took it to the church. At this point we informed the members about what was going on and asked them to pray for Bob and to encourage him as much as they could to turn from his sin. As far as the leaders were concerned, Bob's sin was now public and unrepentant and was bringing the gospel into disrepute. A few weeks after that Bob was removed from our membership. In the early years of his faith, we felt that he was genuinely trying to move away from his sin, despite a few hiccups along the way. But, by the time we had taken the decision to remove him from the church, he was just rolling around in his own moral filth. We kept things private for as long as we could, but then acted decisively when the sin was becoming more public and unrepentant.

(3) Leaders should lead the process and instruct the congregation

In Galatians 6, Paul says that those 'who are spiritual' are called to restore those in sin gently. Sin is deceitful and complex and so leaders need to lead the process because younger sheep can be easily deceived either into sinning, or into accepting sin as not being that bad. We need to teach the sheep about the danger that unchallenged sin can cause to the wider body. If we do not remove people who are in unrepentant sin, then it will be like gangrene and spread throughout the church. That's what Paul talks about in 1 Corinthians 5. Keeping an unrepentant sinner in the church is like leaven that moves through the whole batch.

(4) We need to watch our own hearts

When discipling we need to make sure that it's out of concern for the gospel and not because of hurt feelings or our own reputation. When we've been offended by someone, the danger is that we become hypersensitive to their faults. We lack grace towards that person. We become cynical about them and their motivations. We need to keep soft hearts towards people. Remember, our own hearts are just as prone to sin as anybody else's. Those who have been forgiven much ought to forgive much in return.

(5) Church discipline aims to restore not destroy

We discipline others because we want to see them turn from their sin and be saved. We always say to those we are disciplining that we love them, but we can't affirm their faith while they are acting like this, that we want them to come back and that we will support them if they are repentant. We need to make sure we teach this to every church member. We take no joy in the discipline process. The more public it becomes, the more painful it is. Church discipline is not about self-righteous Christians looking down on those who are inferior to them. At least, it shouldn't be about that. Whenever I publicly announce a matter of discipline to the church, I always remind people that discipline is a good time to look at our owns souls because 1 Corinthians 10:12 reminds us: 'Therefore let anyone who thinks that he stands take heed lest he fall.'

Conclusion

Church discipline can be a difficult and painful process, but it is necessary for the health of the church and the glory of Christ. It can be a heart-breaking experience, but we need to practise it if we are going to see strong, healthy, God-glorifying churches in our communities. I want to end with an extended quote from Robert McCheyne that talks about his change of mind on the benefits of church discipline:

> When I first entered upon the work of the ministry among you, I was exceedingly ignorant of the vast importance of Church discipline. I thought that my great and almost only work was

to pray and preach. I saw your souls to be so precious and the time so short, that I devoted all my time, and care and strength, to labour in word and doctrine. When cases of discipline were brought before me and the elders, I regarded them with something like abhorrence. It was a duty I shrank from; and I may truly say it nearly drove me from the work of the ministry among you altogether. But it pleased God, who teaches His servants in another way than man teaches, to bless some of the cases of discipline to the manifest and undeniable conversion of the souls of those under our care; and from that hour a new light broke in upon my mind, and I saw that if preaching be an ordinance of Christ, so is Church discipline. I now feel very deeply persuaded that both are of God – that two keys are committed to us by Christ: the one the key of doctrine, by means of which we unlock the treasures of the Bible; the other the key of discipline, by which we open or shut the way to the sealing ordinances of the faith. Both are Christ's gift, and neither is to be resigned without sin.[2]

May Christ grant us strength and discernment so that we might honour him in the way we use this important key that the Lord Jesus has entrusted to us.

---

[2] John Whitecross, *The Shorter Catechism Illustrated,* rev. ed. Banner of Truth Trust, 1968.

10. Preaching to the working class

Ian Williamson
Executive Director of Medhurst Ministries

Sunday dinners at Nanna and Grandad Williamson's house are one of my earliest and fondest memories. Three generations – nanna, grandad, mam, dad, brothers, sisters, aunts, uncles and cousins, and occasionally a couple of drunk friends of my dad brought from the pub. Reminiscent of Peter Kay's joke about the emergency chairs, up to 20 family members and friends would be sat around a kitchen table designed for six.[1]

The food was magic, firstly in how it tasted, and secondly, regardless of how many people turned up, there was always enough to go around. Fresh veg from grandad's vegetable garden, a succulent roasted joint of meat and homemade Yorkshire Puddings all smothered with thick onion gravy made with the juice of the roasted joint.

---

1 Peter Kay, *Emergency Chairs at Christmas Dinner*, Live at the Manchester Arena, 24 December 2019. Available at https://www.youtube.com/watch?v=iqBw_Vwxdko. Accessed 22/05/2023.

Story telling

However, what stands out most in my memory isn't the food, the mismatched chairs or even the thick slices of bread that the men used to mop up the leftover gravy. The thing that is ingrained into my memory is the endless and hilarious stories being told around the kitchen table. Whether it was my great aunt Sweary Mary, my grandad or my uncle Al, everyone had a story to tell. And all of them had the gift of making a simple task like going to buy a local newspaper sound like an epic novel. I was fascinated by what they had to say, and I was hooked by their passion, humour and emotion. Similes, metaphors, alliteration and illustrations were skilfully used to transport me and the rest of the audience into the story. When talking about the Big Chute, their social club of choice, I could almost smell the stale beer, hear the raucous laughter and see the blue haze of cigarette smoke.

The working-class storytellers that I grew up with always captured my attention. Even the swearing and foul language contributed to painting the picture, and their mastery of tone meant they rarely caused offence and could even sound poetic. The artistry of the storytellers provoked all kinds of emotions – anger, sympathy, sadness and laughter. The working-class storytellers that I grew up with always captured my heart. Through these stories, I was taught how to live, love and survive on a council estate. From the stories I heard about loyalty, friendship and betrayal to fiddling the Rediffusion and Electric, I learned how to get by on an estate. Then listening to the stories about trade unions, technical colleges and getting a trade, I was taught how to get off the estate. Those working-class storytellers that I grew up with always captured my mind.

The working-class love to tell and listen to stories whether at the kitchen table, in the pub, bait room, hairdresser's, school gate or at church. Yet, sadly, when we go to church, we are more likely to hear a lecture when we should be listening to the most amazing story ever told. In an article on preaching, Gavin Ortlund asks, 'How often have we heard (or preached!) sermons that feel more like a lecture than a sermon – sermons that inform but fail to transform?'.[2] Ortlund answers his own question by claiming that, 'Books on preaching tend to focus on the first, neglecting the equally vital work of contextualisation and application. This imbalance partly explains why much expository preaching fails to speak to the heart.'

The stories around the kitchen table were alluring because they spoke to my heart. The reason for this was they were being told by people like me and featured people like me whose communities and lives were like mine. Not only did I know the actors who were telling and featuring in the stories, the storytellers knew me and the rest of the audience. The best storytellers speak to the heart because they are relational. Take Billy Connolly, for example. Connolly is one of Britain's best-loved stand-up comedians, and he has his audience captured from the start. The reason is he is relational, he relates to his audience and his audience relates to him.

---

[2] Gavin Ortlund and Tim Keller, 'Why Sermons Often Bore' The Gospel Coalition, 5 May 2015. Available at: https://www.thegospelcoalition.org/video/why-sermons-often-bore/. Accessed 22/05/2023.

One example of how he does this is with his joke, 'When the Priest Comes to Visit'. His introduction immediately grabs the audience's attention because they can relate to the story. Even though his story was specific to life as a Catholic in Glasgow, he tells the story in such a way that it is universal for those living in council estates across the UK. Many of his audience wouldn't have had a priest visit the family home when they were children. However, his illustrations provoke memories of being told to be on your best behaviour when an unusual and distinguished guest visits. His other images of life before central heating and double glazing bring back bitter-sweet memories of windows frozen from the inside and having to use coats and jackets at bedtime to supplement the blankets. Connolly is a master of involving you in his story. His description of the bedroom and the children fighting over the jackets reminded me of my childhood growing up on a council estate in England. I felt that I was in that room with him. In fact, he was so gifted with imagery that I felt like he was in my room with me.

Peter Kay is another master of imagery and contextualisation. His comedy series *Phoenix Nights* was about a social club in Bolton. Yet, it resonated with everyone who has experience in a working-class social club, whether in Swansea, Dundee, Gateshead or Romford. Kevin Bridges, another Scottish comedian, tells stories about growing up in Glasgow and his jokes about Space Raiders crisps and 'hoose rice'. Again, it is specific to his life in Glasgow and yet universal to the working class.

These comedians are doing what the storytellers of my childhood did. They do what indigenous preachers immersed in the community do when they are preaching. They hit the mark locally with people exactly like them, and universally with people like them. Their illustrations and punchlines have been experienced and lived out by the comedian and their audience which creates a common bond, camaraderie and trust – something that pastors and preachers need to do with those they are preaching to.

Preachers and pastors who are cultural outsiders, strangers to the town communities and cultures, can learn from working-class storytellers and middle-class comedians like Michael McIntyre. McIntyre has a standard format for his show. When he visits a city like Newcastle, he has no local or cultural link. Therefore, to relate to his audience, he learns about the city's culture and shapes his routine to their context. He will mock local pubs and areas with a dodgy reputation, name-drop and ridicule local celebs and reference local news items. He has the same jokes in every city, yet he makes relevant changes to apply them in different contexts. Therefore, if McIntyre learns the culture and contextualises what he has to say for a joke, how much more should preachers do the same for the sake of salvation.

Jesus contextualised every word, illustration and application in his preaching, and he did this because he knew the people he was preaching to. Jesus lived, worked, and socialised with those to whom he preached. He fished, served, relaxed, worshipped, and went to weddings, funerals, and dinner parties with the people he was preaching to. Reclining with sinners, the religious, the rich, and the poor. Jesus understood everything about the people he preached to, their worldviews, sins, biases, prejudices, hopes, and struggles. He used all he knew about the people and how they lived and spoke.

So, to preach well to the working class, we need to know the working class well; to do this, we need to live alongside them and share our lives with them. It is no good just living near them. We can have a house in the same street yet live in a different world to our neighbours. If every day off work, we visit our parents in another county. Every night off, we meet with friends in the next town, and every time we get a spare hour, we travel 3 miles away from the estate to chill out in a Costa Coffee. If that is what we do, we might as well live on another planet.

If you want to know how the gospel speaks to the lives of the people you preach to, you need to understand the lives of those you preach to. And to do that, you need to reflect Jesus by living alongside the people you preach to. You need to be socialising, working, eating and exercising with them. You need to do whatever you do in and around the people you want to preach to so that you can understand, relate to and apply the word of God to their lives.

Preach so people understand

How well our people understand God's word depends on how well you explain it. In his book *Ministering like the Master*, Stuart Olyott explains how Jesus preached by stating, illustrating and applying.[3] Like Jesus, when preaching to the working class, you need to explain the Bible fully, every book, chapter and verse. You do not have to stick to parables or the gospels to preach to the working class; we need to hear the whole counsel of God. Don't short-change us. We need all of it. 2 Timothy 3:16–17 says that 'All Scripture is God-breathed and is useful for teaching, rebuking, correcting and training in righteousness, so that the servant of God may be thoroughly equipped for every good work.' You also need to explain it simply – as it says in 2 Corinthians 4:2, 'by setting forth the truth plainly we commend ourselves to everyone's conscience in the sight of God.'

Explaining the Bible thoroughly yet simply is essential, regardless of who you preach to. It is not because we can't understand profound theological truths. It is because if you can't explain it simply, then we will know that you need to understand the text better and that you need to work harder. Have you ever had a child ask you about something that you know but can't explain? Sometimes when my children ask me a question, I can get frustrated because although I know the answer, I don't understand it well enough to teach it. Sometimes we can be like that when preaching. We might grasp something but not well enough to explain it, so we waffle on or use theological terms and hope that people will stay quiet and not ask questions. Explaining something simply is not dumbing it down. It takes skill and effort. The council estate storytellers of my youth knew their stories and were skilful in telling them.

---

[3] Stuart Olyott, *Ministering Like the Master: Three Messages for Today's Preachers,* The Banner of Truth Trust, 2003.

Similarly, preachers need to understand the word of God and be proficient in how they preach. As Paul says to Timothy, 'Do your best to present yourself to God as one approved, a worker who does not need to be ashamed and who correctly handles the word of truth' (2 Tim. 2:15).

The best example of preaching simply and skilfully is Jesus. Stuart Olyott reminds us, 'Our Lord's way of speaking was distinctive, clear, plain and easy to copy.'[4] Someone who can preach simply and skilfully won't presume that we know what they are talking about. If you use words like 'propitiation' and 'sanctification', explain what they mean. Otherwise, we might switch off and spend the sermon wondering what the word 'genealogy' means and miss that Jesus died for our sins. If you presume we know what you are talking about, you risk losing us.

Yet similarly, don't presume we are ignorant and don't know what you're talking about. Too many preachers take the stance of a Year 5 teacher and talk down to us. Coming out with things like, 'Today we're going to learn about a big word called "eschatology". Does anybody know what that means?' Our churches are full of boffins in disguise, and I admit some have worked hard at looking like fools. Still, most of us love to read and listen to sermons online; our congregations are gifted and bright as a button, so make every effort to avoid offending them. To preach well to the working class, we need to engage them with our preaching.

---

4 Olyott, *Ministering Like the Master*.

Preach with illustrations

Jesus is the master of illustrations and used everything his audience experienced to illuminate his Word. This helped his hearers to understand the passage intellectually whilst motivating them to do something in response.

Olyott says that Jesus did this because everything becomes plain once a word picture is lodged in a person's mind.[5] Bryan Chapell tells us that illustrations are not for the head so much as the heart. They don't primarily explain; they motivate. They get the hearer thinking about how the passage is relevant to their life and how they should respond to this passage. They prepare our hearts for and provide a bridge to the application.[6]

For family devotions, we used to use the Urban Catechism. It was my children's favourite devotions as it kept their attention. One of the passages we looked at explained how as unbelievers, we suppress the truth of God (Rom. 1:18–20):

> The wrath of God is being revealed from heaven against all the godlessness and wickedness of people, who suppress the truth by their wickedness, since what may be known about God is plain to them, because God has made it plain to them. For since the creation of the world, God's invisible qualities – his eternal power and divine nature – have been clearly seen, being understood from what has been made, so that people are without excuse.

---

5 Olyott, *Ministering Like the Master*.
6 Bryan Chapell, *Christ Centered Preaching*, ebook, Apple Books, 2006 p. 159.

Sermons From The Schemes

And there was an illustration given to explain how we suppress the truth. It talks about how suppressing the truth is like pushing a ball under the water in the swimming pool – eventually, it pops back up. A bit like suppressing the truth of God; we can pretend he doesn't exist and try and push him out of view. But we can't force him under for long as we will be reminded of him every time we see his creation, trees, babies being born, etc.

We were swimming in the local pool several months after reading that devotion. Esther and Hannah were trying to push a beach ball under the water, and they both shouted, 'Dad, we are trying to suppress the truth like in Romans.' Illustrations help the sermon become a personal conversation and will engage the congregation like my children were with the catechism. The illustration helped my kids to understand the Bible, stay interested in what I was teaching them and remember what I had taught them.

There are several ways of illustrating the text using other Bible passages and quotes from authors or theologians. Still, the personal story best fits the working-class context. Having good illustrations that you know well and can memorise is also helpful for preachers, especially those who heavily rely on their notes. Memorising your illustrations lets the preacher get personal with the hearers by taking a break from looking at their notes and keeping eye contact with the congregation.

Application is the personal consequence of the truth the Scripture presents. It answers the question, 'So what?' How often has a sermon finished and left you thinking, what has that got to do with me, my marriage, family, illness and life today in the UK? 'Do not merely listen to the word, and so deceive yourselves. Do what it says' (Jas. 1:22).

Sermon applications should be provocative and leave the hearer knowing how to respond to God's word, practically and spiritually. When teaching about application, Chapell reminds his students of the Westminster Standards and the third catechism question which asks, 'What do the Scriptures principally teach?' The answer is, 'The Scriptures principally teach what man is to believe concerning God and what duty God requires of man.' It concludes with, 'Explanation is what man is to believe concerning God. Application is what duty God requires of man.'[7]

The storytellers around the dinner table not only explained that money could be made from fiddling the Electric and Rediffusion, they also helped me apply what I had learned by describing how a strategically placed butter knife would release an abundance of fifty pence pieces from the meter. If these working-class orators prepared me for council estate life, how much more should an orator of God's word prepare the hearer for a godly life.

I grew up without a father and struggled to navigate the transition from boyhood to manhood. I was given a book about the birds and the bees – a book about the facts of life, without the instructions to live it. When I grew facial hair, I was prepared for that – I knew that I had to shave. The problem was I didn't know how to shave. I needed more than just the facts.

---

[7] Chapell, *Christ Centered Preaching,* p. 3.

I also needed someone to help me practically apply what I had learned. Unfortunately, that help never came. It took months of razor burns, cuts and wonky sideburns before I knew what I was doing. When preaching to the working class, you must help apply the word of God to our lives. Enabling your listeners to leave the church service informed and equipped to avoid the cuts and razor burns of council estate life.

Learning from, listening to and living with the working class is essential if you want to effectively explain, illustrate and apply the word of God to their lives. However, remember that it is only by the Holy Spirit that your hearers will be able and willing to be transformed by anything you say. That is why before you preach to the working class, you must also pray with and for them. Preaching, regardless of who you're preaching to, should be understood as relational. First between the preacher and God, then between the preacher and his congregation, and the reason for preaching itself, the relationship between God and the listeners.

11. Abuse and the gospel

Mez McConnell
Pastor of Niddrie Community Church, Edinburgh,
and Director of 20schemes

During the early years of my childhood abuse, I gave up on God. I had huge questions which nobody could answer. Where was God when it was all happening? Why did he let people torture, beat and starve me? Why wouldn't he stop it? Did he care? Was he even there?

My road to faith was long, slow and painful. And who would have thought that it would be the doctrine of PSA that has most encouraged and comforted me over the years as I've tried to process my pain? Many believers probably don't even know what PSA is. It's a doctrine that has fallen out of fashion and has taken a bit of a kicking from liberals for being nothing more than cosmic child abuse. To appreciate what Jesus has done for us we need to work hard at understanding PSA.

Let me give you a brief definition.

> The doctrine of penal substitutionary atonement states that God gave himself in the person of his Son to suffer instead of sinful humanity the death, punishment and curse due to us as the penalty for sin.

It's not just a doctrine for professors and boffins. It's for all of us – especially the hurting and those who have been abused. It is controversial and there are various atonement models out there but here I am sticking with PSA. I just want to outline 12 reasons why I believe it, and how it can bring comfort to bruised and battered souls.

(1) PSA demonstrates that all people are sinners – even the abused

I'd played the victim card for so long that it was like a slap in the mush when I was first confronted with my sin. If anybody needed God's wrath it was them, my abusers, right? Me? I needed a break. I needed understanding. I'd suffered after all. In my mind, all the crap that had happened to me excused all my sinful, selfish behaviour. But the Bible is clear. *All have sinned and fall short of the glory of God* (Rom. 3:23). That includes the paedo, the rapist, the bully, the doctor, the working man, the single mum, the people who've worked hard all their lives and have loved their kids, you and me. We are all lawbreakers and rebels against the rule of a holy God. That's a bitter pill to swallow but once its down it begins to do its work of slowly healing the broken spirited.

(2) PSA helps us understand why the world is the way it is

Why was always my biggest question. Why are you doing this to me? Why is this happening? PSA teaches us the reason why Jesus had to come and suffer and answers our whys. Evil happens because our world is broken and sick. Not as broken and evil as it could be – but it's a mess. You don't send a mop and bucket to clean up an oil tanker spillage. It's a big mess that needs a huge clean-up operation. The same for our sin-stricken world. Why did Jesus go through so much? Why would God put him through all of that? Because we need to realise the size of our sin problem. The clean-up job was huge.

People who question PSA to ask why God would go so over the top in his punishment really don't appreciate just how sick and depraved our world really is. Only the Bible offers us a coherent worldview of the Fall and how sin entered this world and destroyed everything. That's more comfort than all the meaningless, 'survival of the fittest' type of stuff. You know, the people who say it was all a Big Bang and there's no real meaning. Really? Well, let's shut up shop then and do what we like. None of it means anything. Not your suffering, nor mine. But the fact that we suffer from depression and anxiety and stress and worry and shame and guilt shows that we instinctively know that life has to have meaning. It must have.

Why do parents abuse their kids? Husbands their wives, wives their husbands? Why commit such depraved acts on the weak and defenceless and vulnerable? Sin is the reason why. A world handed over to its own carnal, sick desires. Some of us are not only the fruit of that, we also contribute to it too!

(3) PSA offers us hope – meaningful hope

God so loved the world – despite all its filth and perversion – that he sent his only Son. God didn't leave us with some cryptic clues and hope we'd find him. God as man came to find us. For many of us, hope has been snuffed out. I'd hoped for years my dad would meet another woman, and he did, but by that time it had been 10 years, and by the time I was 14, I was hardened and cynical. Too scared to hope, for it was always proved wrong and ruthlessly crushed by a boot or a broom handle.

So, when I heard that Jesus had come and what he went through, hope swelled again. Slowly, tentatively. I wanted to make sure it was real. It all sounded a little too good to be true. But, when I found Jesus, I mean I really found him, really understood the depths he went to in order to rescue me, I hung on to him for dear life. I am nothing without Jesus. My life is nothing without Jesus. And that's the greatest and safest place to be on the planet. Trust me on that. Don't take my word for it. The Bible tells us to trust and see that the Lord is good. I can tell you a piece of pie is good, but you'll only ever know for yourself if you eat a piece. In Jesus, there is real hope, meaningful hope and once you have it, you want to keep it. And the good news is you can have it.

(4) PSA is the answer to our *whys* and *whats*

His death is the answer to our *whys* and *whats*. Why doesn't God help us? What is he doing when I'm being tortured and terrified?

Jesus lived as a man. He's not sat on his throne in heaven going, *'That's a shame.'* He entered our reality. God contracted to a span's width, incomprehensibly made man. He didn't leave us to stew in our mess. He jumped right in the crapper with us. The answer to many of our questions isn't found in the fact that he came – but in the manner of his coming, his living, his dying and his leaving. Jesus was stone cold abused. Jesus suffered terrors at the hands of cruel, twisted, evil, bitter men. He endured suffering, so much so that *'Where was he when...?'* questions become *'Why would he do that for a person like me?'* questions.

(5) PSA reminds me that our God is compassionate and understands our pain

When I was a kid, I was locked in rooms and cupboards, often beaten without mercy. When I was ill, I would be beaten further. If I was prescribed medicine from the doctor, my mother would bin it and tell me to suck it up. She once beat me and stamped on me for having appendicitis, and even when I wound up in hospital, she would visit me to threaten me and tell me what torture she had planned when I got out. Zero compassion. Zero love. And then I learned about Jesus and how compassion oozed out of every pore! Compassion on the poor, the downtrodden, the neglected. This is not some distant

God of Greek mythology, but a God who draws near and shares our pain. It doesn't end my pain, but it gives me a measure of comfort that Jesus understands more than I think he does.

Make no mistake, Jesus is grieved at how many of us have been treated and how all of us treat others. Jesus is not only listening and caring, but he is also experiencing too. He hurts for the powerlessness of the helpless. The children hiding under the tables while their Ma is being kicked up and down. For innocents passed around paedophile rings. The sex offender sat in his cell wondering how on earth he got there. Jesus knows. But he doesn't just stop at sympathy and compassion. On the cross, he does something about it.

(6) PSA reminds me that our suffering is awful, but our spiritual state is far more dangerous

Of course, Jesus had compassion on people for their troubles, but Matthew 9:36 shows us that Jesus' compassion spilled over onto the crowds because they were *like sheep without a shepherd*. Imagine the secret pains and the abuse sufferers and abusers in those crowds – and yet Jesus grieved over the state of their souls. The biggest issue facing people in the world today is their lostness, not just their pain. There is something far worse than the pain, shame, humiliation and indignity of abuse, and that is to spend eternity separated from God. Abuse breaks his heart, but the spiritual blindness of humans pierced the depths of his soul, even unto his bloody, brutal death.

(7) PSA reminds me that Jesus was humiliated more

PSA reminds me that even in my most degrading and humiliating moments, Jesus was humiliated more. The perfect, sinless God-Man spat on by his creation. Punched and kicked and jeered at. Stripped and crucified. An innocent man beaten and mocked for the amusement of others. He knows humiliation alright. I think back to being stripped naked as a child and humiliated so cruelly, and as I look to the cross, I see the tears of him who suffered his own humiliation far, far greater than mine.

(8) PSA reminds me that Jesus knows the same rejection I knew

All we want as kids is to be loved. I never heard those words. Ever. Not once as a child. Not once from a parent in my 46 years. I was passed from foster home to foster home, and kids home to kids home. Never feeling wanted, always feeling rejected. Then I committed the cardinal sin of being smart. So, my estate pals couldn't cope that I went to a grammar school, and my grammar school classmates couldn't cope that I came from an estate. Yet we read in John 1:11 that Jesus came to his own, but his own people did not receive him. Even his own family weren't having it about Jesus. Some of them thought he'd lost it. Even the Samaritans rejected him on his way to Jerusalem. And you would have thought the Samaritans would have known better, given that everyone looked down on them.

(9) PSA puts our pain and suffering in perspective

It doesn't lessen it, but Isaiah 53:3 is a special verse. 'He was despised and rejected by mankind, a man of suffering, and familiar with pain. Like one from whom people hide their faces he was despised, and we held him in low esteem.' We say we know pain, and many of us do. But we have no real comprehension of the agonies of the cross. Crucifixion was an awful way to go out. Being flogged with a bone-tipped whip tearing out chunks of his flesh. Beaten and bloody with his poor Ma watching as the crowds baited him. Any slight movements causing untold excruciating pain. The blood loss. His lungs collapsing as he basically suffocates to death. Then feeling the full wrath of the Father being poured out upon him – a wrath we will never have to face if we are trusting in Christ. We shouldn't minimise our pain but we should put it into perspective in order to stop us becoming trapped and bitter in our misery.

(10) All of Jesus' pain, suffering and humiliation was *voluntary*

As a child, I was dragged kicking and screaming by my hair, punished remorselessly for any minor infringement, including not turning the TV over quickly enough (the day before remotes, kids). I was forced to lie on the floor with my mouth forced open while adults took it in turns to spit in my mouth. I was urinated on for laughs. Not to mention the sexual abuse, the starvation, the isolation and the neglect. I was even beaten if caught reading a book. All of it outside of my control. All of it by people bigger and stronger than me, who were supposed to love and protect me. This is not what is happening when Jesus goes to the cross. This is not an angry father dragging his poor, innocent son off to get an absolute hiding and then mercilessly watching his die slowly.

And the main reason we know for a fact why PSA is not cosmic child abuse is found in John 10:

> I am the good shepherd. The good shepherd lays down his life for the sheep (Jn. 10:11).

> Just as the Father knows me and I know the Father – and I lay down my life for the sheep (Jn. 10:15).

> The reason my Father loves me is that I lay down my life – only to take it up again (Jn. 10:17).

But the absolute clincher, beyond all doubt is found in verse 18:

> No one takes it from me, but I lay it down of my own accord. I have authority to lay it down and authority to take it up again.

In other words, unlike many of us, Jesus volunteered to be abused, suffer and die. As he dies, the full wrath of God is unleashed upon him. In the moment he cries, 'It is finished,' he feels like the Father has deserted, forsaken and forgotten him. As a Man, he knew the true pain of separation. He who knew no sin was made sin. Cursed like a criminal, paedo, rapist, junkie, burglar, doctor, lawyer, you, me. In that act he takes upon himself the punishment we deserve. Why? To satisfy the justice of God. I would have done anything to escape my pain, my suffering and abuse, but Jesus literally walked into the fires of hell for us. He wasn't dragged to the cross kicking and screaming. He knew what he had come to do and he did it out of obedience and love for the Father. That is not cosmic child abuse. That is cosmic love. That is love on a scale none of us can imagine, even those of us who grew up happy with both parents.

(11) PSA reminds us that justice will ultimately be served

PSA reminds us that we may not get justice in this life. But one day it will ultimately be served – either by the sinner, or, for the believer, by Jesus. My abusers are dead, mostly. The others I can't even remember their names. I regret that I never pursued justice, and so I trust when they met with God, it was served. But, sometimes in a fallen world, even when we pursue justice, we don't get it. The world and the law are imperfect, stained by sin. At that point, because vengeance is closed to the Christian, we must leave it in the hands of God who will have his ultimate justice. Listen, if God pursued justice in the death of his Son, how much more will he pursue it on unrepentant sinners? PSA gives me a measure of comfort, knowing that the God of all the earth will ultimately do right. And hard as it is, I must rest in that.

Maybe you're good for nothing. An abuser. A manipulator. A liar. A deceiver. Playing the game in public but a monster behind closed doors. Maybe you think you're getting away with it. Even coming to church and saying how sorry you are but never really changing. And the people you are manipulating and dominating are too scared to out you. Let me tell you, your time will come. One day you will stand before God and give an account. He's not fooled by your flattery and deception and smooth words. You will go to hell. As will all people who refuse to bow the knee to King Jesus and allow him to change their hearts and their lives. You can't be claiming to be a Christian when you're knocking your missus about. Or you're abusing the kids. Or you're manipulating and dominating your partner at home. Just because you may have gotten away with it for a long time doesn't mean you will always get away with it. Mark my words, it is a terrible thing to fall into the hands of Almighty God. And if you think you will somehow get off on a technicality for lack of evidence then think again. He sent his own Son to suffer and to die to satisfy his holy justice against sin. You're deluded if you think you will escape him.

But ... if we bow the knee to Jesus, our sin debt is paid. It has been forgiven. Whoever we are and whatever we have done. I admit, I don't like the thought of that for child abusers and others. But it is the truth and it is not for me to judge who is worthy and who is not. Again, that is the scandal of grace.

(12) PSA reminds me of 1 Corinthians 1:26-29

> Not many of you were wise by human standards; not many were influential; not many were of noble birth. But God chose the foolish things of the world to shame the wise; God chose the weak things of the world to shame the strong. God chose

> the lowly things of this world and the despised things – and things that are not – to nullify the things that are, so that no one may boast before him (1 Cor. 1:26–29).

You may be broken right now – damaged, useless, for that's how you were made to feel. Maybe you look in the mirror and hate what you see. God uses the useless, fearful, broken, despised, weak and foolish. He even uses the formerly, truly evil people – because that's what we all are until we turn from our sins and throw ourselves on Christ's mercy. And that wrath that rests on us is transferred to him, and we are forgiven, accepted and clean. Maybe family and friends will take time to be convinced if you've done a lot of damage over the years. But God can take the hardest heart and the most crushed spirit and breathe new life into both if there is genuine repentance and a willingness to walk in obedience to his Word. Thank God for his grace. Thank God for his mercy. Thank God for his justice. Thank God for his forgiveness. Thank God for reconciliation. Thank God for Jesus. Thank God for the gospel.

12. Addictions

Mez McConnell
Pastor of Niddrie Community Church, Edinburgh,
and Director of 20schemes

This is one of the biggest issues of our ministry. We deal with an almost never-ending flow of addicts in the church. Let me recommend some books to you: *Addictions: A Banquet in The Grave* by Ed Welch; *Blame It on The Brain?* by Ed Welch; *The Crossroads: A Step by Step Guide Away From Addiction* by Ed Welch.[1]

The topic is controversial in many church circles. Many pastors have no clue what to do with a drug addict. They just hope the doctor is prescribing some medication for them or maybe they send them to a counsellor or encourage them to go to an AA or NA meeting. Some of the more switched-on

---

1 Ed Welch, *Addictions: A Banquet in The Grave, Finding Hope in the Power of the Gospel,* Presbyterian and Reformed, 2001; Ed Welch, *Blame It on The Brain? Distinguishing Chemical Imbalances, Brain Disorders, and Disobedience,* Presbyterian and Reformed, 1998; Ed Welch, *The Crossroads: A Step by Step Guide Away From Addiction,* New Growth Press, 2008.

churches set up their own specific groups for addicts but most of the material on offer is a combination of worldly wisdom and patched together Bible verses, at best. The big debate in this area is around the fact that the whole 'addiction as disease' model that is widespread in the medical profession is taken as gospel by many people working in our areas, including churches. This view teaches that addicts cannot help themselves. Their problem is they have a disease or an illness.

Now, let's be clear, the Bible does use the language of disease and illness when it comes to describing the spiritual condition of humanity. In fact, some of the best-known passages in Scripture use the imagery of sickness and healing:

> Your whole head is injured; your whole heart is afflicted. From the sole of your foot to the top of your head there is no soundness – only wounds and welts and open sores, not cleansed or bandaged or soothed with oil (Is. 1:5-6).

> But he was pierced for our transgressions, he was crushed for our iniquities; the punishment that brought us peace was on him, and by his wounds we are healed (Is. 53:5).

The Bible clearly says that sin has many things in common with a disease. For example, it affects our entire being, it is painful and it leads to death. Some people take these verses and run with them as proof that addiction is a disease. But the problem is that the Bible also uses other language to describe addiction and we must take *all* of what the Bible says into consideration before we build a theology on it. It is an oversimplification to say that all addiction is simply an illness. So, let's look at some of the words and phrases the Bible uses.

Addiction is sin

When Solomon wrote Proverbs 23:29-35, he was talking about the way of the foolish man and the sinful choices he was making. In Paul's letter to the Galatians 5:19-21 he says that drunkenness is no different to sexual immorality, thievery or selfish ambition. It is all equally immoral. It is all sin. So that means that addictions are not just illnesses that we pick up like the common cold, but they are proactive choices that harm not just our relationships with each other but, more importantly, our relationship with God.

Addiction is idolatry

Simply put, an addict desires the creation rather than the creator. 'Who will you worship?' is a question that is constantly asked in the Bible. The Old Testament consists of God constantly calling his people to repent of the idolatry in their midst. The Ten Commandments also focus on the theme of idolatry. The greatest command is not to have any gods before the one, true God:

> You shall have no other gods before me. You shall not make for yourself an image in the form of anything in heaven above or on the earth beneath or in the waters below. You shall not bow down to them or worship them; for I, the LORD your God, am a jealous God, punishing the children for the sin of the

parents to the third and fourth generation of those who hate me, but showing love to a thousand generations of those who love me and keep my commandments (Deut. 5:7-10).

It's important to remember that idolatry in the Old Testament was not just about bowing down to statues. It was deliberate moves away from worshipping God to worshipping something or someone else. In the New Testament we also have this theme of idols. At the end of 1 John 5 he writes this: 'Dear children, keep yourselves from idols.' John's letter never mentions physical idols, but he says this in 1 John 2:15-16: 'Do not love the world or anything in the world. If anyone loves the world, love for the Father is not in them. For everything in the world – the lust of the flesh, the lust of the eyes, and the pride of life – comes not from the Father but from the world.'

John is concerned with the hidden idols of the heart, not physical ones made by hands. In other words, Scripture allows us to widen our definition of what idols are. Therefore, idolatry includes anything we worship. It's about what we set our affections on. It's about the lusts of the flesh, the lust of the eyes and the pride of life. So, an idolater may well worship Buddha, but they may also lust after pleasure, respect, love, power, control or freedom from pain. The problem is not the things around us but the false worship of the heart.

The point of idolatry is that the thing worshipped makes the person feel good, at least initially. We drink because it's fun at first. It's an escape from our boring lives. Maybe we take drugs to forget a painful situation. We self-harm. We watch porn. It starts off as enjoyable. We have created something we think we are in control of. But soon we lose control. The thing we used to be in charge of is now taking over our life. It doesn't feel so good anymore, so we do more of whatever it is that is controlling us to get that good feeling back. Now we are quickly moving on to be dominated by our idol. Now we *need* it to function. If you look at the prophets of Baal on Mount Carmel in 1 Kings 18, they did everything to manipulate Baal to do their will. They danced and prayed and slashed themselves to get Baal to do what they wanted. The addict wants the idol to do their will and give them what they want. They want these activities to give them good feelings or a sense of power or whatever their heart is craving.

The problem with idolatry is that it doesn't cooperate. Rather than us mastering our idols, our idols master us. Why do these idols have such power over us? It's because Satan is working behind the scenes! As Ephesians 6:12 tells us: 'For our struggle is not against flesh and blood,' – or alcohol and drugs – 'but against the rulers, against the authorities, against the powers of this dark world and against the spiritual forces of evil in the heavenly realms.'

Now some of you may be wondering if there is a difference between a person addicted to alcohol and one addicted to work. Is there a difference between someone addicted to drugs or to power? Yes and no. No, because we all have idols – but, yes, because some idols specifically hook our bodily passions and desires. This group of addictions includes drugs, alcohol, sexual sin and food. These idolatries can provide physical pleasure, relieve physical tension and soothe physical desires. Such payoffs can be difficult to resist. Our physical desires are very strong pulls. And Satan loves this because if something feels good, then you can bet your life on it that he will twist this thing and take advantage of it in your life. God has created us with physical needs and desires which, kept within appropriate limits by a heart of faith, can lead to pleasure. Satan wants to overturn God's order and have physical desires rule the person.

> For the addict dope is God. It is the supreme being, the Higher Power, in the junkie's life. He is subjugated to its will. He follows its commandments. The drug is the definition of happiness, and gives the meaning of love. Each shot of junk in his veins is a shot of divine love, and it makes the addict feel resplendent with the grace of God.[2]

So, are people walking into our church going, 'I have a problem with idolatry, Mez, what can you do to help me mate?' Obviously not. Because what I am describing is a biblical definition. It is deeply spiritual and biblical. And all addicts are blind. All sinners are blind to the truths of God's word. Sin is by its very nature hidden and the addict doesn't see their idolatry. That's why we need the Lord Jesus to break people's addictions. No amount of screaming, threats, tears, or pleading (from mums) will stop an addict. They need the power of God to free the soul.

Addiction, in whatever form, violates the command 'You shall have no other gods before me' (Ex. 20:3). For example,

---

2 B. Meehan, *Beyond the Yellow Brick Road,* Contemporary Books, 1984, p. 175, quoted in Edward T. Welch, *Addictions: A Banquet in the Grave: Finding Hope in the Power of the Gospel,* P&R Publishing, 2001, p. 53.

heavy drinkers love alcohol. Someone who struggles with pornography loves sex. A drug user loves drugs. They are controlled by it as if they were its subjects. And all idolatry is self-worship. We worship people and things to get what we want. Those who worship money do so to get what they want. Addicts do not do things to glorify God or love their neighbour. They are addicts for their own desires. If you look at a drug addict, for example, they will spend all their time getting what they need to satisfy their desires – they will not let friends, family or even their own children get in the way of what they want. So, to say that an addiction is a disease is false because an idol is something we create to serve us. An idol is something we manipulate for our own selfish desires. But then it ends up enslaving us and controlling our lives.

Addiction is slavery to sin

The Bible teaches us that sin is a binding power that wants to control and enslave us. Martin Luther wrote a very important book on this subject called *The Bondage of the Will*. In it, he emphasised that our will is powerless apart from the power and grace of God poured out on us. Sin is more than a conscious choice. Sin controls us (Jn. 8:34). It captures and overtakes us (Gal. 6:1). In fact, there are times when we intend to do one thing, but sin causes us to do things we don't want to do. Sin feels exactly like a disease sometimes (Rom. 7:15–17). The main difference between slavery to sin and a disease is that we are responsible for our slavery, whereas the disease model makes us helpless victims.

> Man ... does not do evil against his will, under pressure, as though he were taken by the scruff of the neck and dragged into it, like a thief ... being dragged off against his will to punishment; but he does it spontaneously and voluntarily. And this willingness or volition is something which he cannot in his own strength eliminate, restrain, or alter (Martin Luther).[3]
>
> All sin is simultaneously pitiable slavery and overt rebelliousness or selfishness (Ed Welch).[4]

In other words, we are slaves to our sin, but we are also responsible for it at the same time. Therefore, we need the Lord Jesus. We need to admit that we are sinners (that *we* have caused our own mess, no one else) and that we can only find forgiveness, healing and redemption in Jesus Christ. He alone offers the power to cast off sin.

Addiction is adultery

Proverbs 7:6-23 paints us a picture of a young man getting his groove on with a hooker. It helps us understand how he is making decisions and how he is being sucked in by his own foolish, sinful desires. The language used is one of adultery.

That sense of being controlled and being dominated by another, the lies and the obsession with another. Listen to an addict:

---

[3] Martin Luther, *The Bondage of the Will,* published in English, 1823.
[4] Welch, *Addictions: A Banquet in the Grave,* p. 34.

> [My wife] said to me that I was going to have to make a choice – either cocaine or her. Before she finished the sentence, I knew what was coming, so I told her to think carefully about what she was going to say. It was clear to me that there wasn't a choice. I love my wife, but I'm not going to choose anything over cocaine. It's sick, but that's what things have come to. Nothing and nobody comes before my coke.[5]

Think about the young man in Proverbs 7. The tale of this young man starts innocently enough. He is just walking along the street. However, there is intention in his footsteps. He purposefully goes to the street near her corner (verse 8). He goes at dusk when he knows she will be there. And she talks sweetly to him and beckons him. Then he has his pleasure for the moment, but it doesn't end well (verses 22–23). How does this apply to the addict? It gives us more personal language to describe addiction. Addicts indulge in a secret life that will eventually be exposed. Deception is commonplace. People are unfaithful to those around them and love the substance. They do it because they desire the substance more than anything else. The relationship with the substance becomes their life. But why? It all seems so foolish. There is no satisfactory answer. Sin is not rational. It doesn't make sense. It doesn't look into the future. It doesn't consider the consequences, especially if they are not immediate. All it knows is, '*I want more.*'

---

5 Welch, *Addictions: A Banquet in the Grave,* p. 56.

Addiction is foolishness

Another theme that overlaps with idolatry and adultery is foolishness. The book of Proverbs is a book about Wisdom and Folly. Folly is characterised as thoughtlessness and decisions to pursue a course that is briefly pleasurable but ultimately painful. Sin makes us stupid, not intellectually but morally.

> They [idolaters] know nothing, they understand nothing; their eyes are plastered over so they cannot see, and their minds closed so they cannot understand ... [He] feeds on ashes; a deluded heart misleads him (Is. 44:18, 20).

The fool's attention wanders. He ignores all consequences. He is persuaded that his way is the right way. He thinks he will get away from it. He goes with his feelings, not realising that they can mislead. He ignores the way of wisdom. The bottom line is that addiction is complicated and cannot be explained away easily. But one thing is for certain: it is not a disease. Biblically speaking, addiction is a sin or sins that are idolatrous (in other words something we worship), sins that enslave us, and sins that cause us to make foolish decisions in pursuit of something we know is destroying us.

Practical helps

If we come with this understanding of addiction, it can help us in several ways as we cope with those in our midst.

(1) Know that addiction is a choice – and, therefore, don't blame anybody else. An addiction is something that, somewhere along the line, we chose. It's not like one day a person is walking

along and then they suddenly fell onto a needle full of heroin. Were they born with the innate desire to max out all the credit cards on clothes? No, it's a choice. All sin is a choice at its root. It is purposeful and self-conscious. The issue becomes more complicated when that choice turns into an out-of-control addiction. Is it still a choice or has it become a disease? The Bible says at this point a person has become double-minded. They hate what they do, and they love what they do. Even with all the associated misery, people stay with their addictions on some level because their addiction does something for them. It serves them. It may allow a brief opportunity to forget, punish, cure self-consciousness, avoid pain, fill holes in a self-image, manage emotions, fit in with others, keep loneliness at bay. It's not to deny the reality of being taken captive by an addictive substance but just to say that for the addict, slavery with the object of desire is something preferable to freedom without it. This is not the same as a disease.

There is this culture in our society that feeds into victim mentality. If we blame others for our addictions, then we will end up bitter and will simply remain stuck in bondage. Instead we need to acknowledge that the way of freedom is found in Jesus Christ alone. That doesn't mean that it gets easier after making that decision; it can be harder. However, the path of the Lord Jesus brings life. So in following Jesus, people need to take responsibility for their actions. We do people no favours by making excuses for their choices and sin. We are not saying don't empathise. But we are saying that we need to understand the big issues biblically if we ever want to help people.

(2) Know that the problems that an addict faces are very serious, but they are common to everybody. Addicts aren't special because, at heart, we are all addicts. We all chase after sinful pleasures. It may not be drink and drugs, but it may be money, sex and power. We may make an idol out of our job and our families. That's why we need to repent of any judgementalism. If we are working with addicts, then we will have sinned against them in our attitudes at some point because it can be very frustrating! We need to be patient and keeping pointing people towards the Lord Jesus.

(3) We need to show people the seriousness of their problems. But we need to hold out the hope of the gospel. Because it is sin, there is a cure in Jesus. And when we come to Jesus we can be helped completely if we submit to his lordship.

(4) Don't make false promises to people. This means that change is a process. Problems don't go away overnight. But it is as we make good choices in response to the Spirit's work in our lives that we change. We won't reach perfection until we meet Christ and so, before that happens, our walk with the Lord is a constant battle against sin and our addictions. But the battle does get easier as we walk in step with the Spirit.

(5) We need to pray for discernment in our ministries. Most serious drug users and alcoholics and gamblers are inveterate liars. They learn the language of Zion very quickly and we must be careful in our discipleship that we are not importing a form of morality. When we were first working with addicts, we used to say to them, 'Why don't you come down 5mg of methadone a week?' We'd set them little targets in terms of

their discipleships. But they failed and got really discouraged and we realized that, inadvertently, we'd been heaping burdens on them and that led them into a downward spiral.

(6) Be realistic about the battle ahead. Prepare them for failure and hard work. The spiritual life is a battle. As Ed Welch says, 'The only possible attitude towards out-of-control desires is all out war.'[6] Jesus tells us, 'If your hand or your foot causes you to stumble, cut it off and throw it away' (Mt. 18:8). War sharpens the senses, especially when the enemy constantly hides. We stay vigilant. The problem is that we often forget that we are in a war. We forget we are in a constant spiritual battle. Spiritual battles are very different to physical ones. Spiritual issues tend to hide. We need to declare war. We need to move from vacation mode to being alert and battle.

(7) We need to exhort people to self-control. Self-control is not for the faint hearted. It is very difficult, and it takes a mean streak. Being a Christian means that we must make good, consistent decisions in small and big things. This is hard. When was the last time you said 'no' to something out of obedience to Christ? Maybe you can say 'no' to cocaine, but you struggle to say 'no' to looking at a sexually provocative advertisement? Maybe you can say 'no' to that, but you can't say 'no' to a second or third drink? It's hard to say 'no'. Especially when we think we are getting away with our decisions. But God knows all things and see all things. And that which is in the darkness will come out in the light.

---

6 Welch, *Addictions: A Banquet in the Grave*, p. 226.

We need to persevere. There is grace for every battle. We can win in this battle because we know there is one who has already defeated sin and death, and this is Christ. We need to remember that and run to his grace again and again.

13. Women's ministry and the Word:
Trust God's word as sufficient for all circumstances and situations

Sharon Dickens
Director of Women's Ministry, 20Schemes

I'm asked two things on a regular basis. First, can you tell me about a helpful book for women who are struggling with purity, singleness, miscarriage, mental health, body image ... the list is endless. And, secondly, can you tell me some helpful verses I can send to someone who is struggling with such and such.

In fact, I remember recently being asked for book recommendations and I suggested a book of the Bible that lady in question might study and she went to someone else on the team and got a couple of Christian lifestyle book recommendations. To be honest, even though this did make me laugh out loud, there was a part of me that just paused and reflected. It was disconcerting. We have become so used to and reliant on using external resources as our main source of help for the women's discipleship. I stopped and asked myself, 'Have we forgotten the sufficiency of God's word?'

I've been dwelling on this for months and I'd planned to write a wee blog, ranting about it, hoping to get it out of my system. The blog might not have materialised but the thoughts haven't left me. Don't get me wrong, there are a ton of amazing resources out there that are biblical, robust and seriously helpful. We've written a few ourselves at 20schemes, like the *First Steps Series* or *Unexceptional* (which is currently being translated into Spanish – still blows my mind every time I think about that). But when it comes to the discipleship of women, have we become too reliant on them? Are books the first thing we reach for? Have we forgotten the depth of wisdom and truth we have at hand in the infallible word of God? Do we really trust God's word as sufficient for all circumstances and situations that we come across? If we are being honest, our heads may believe that, but our action may display a different truth.

As we focus on the Word, and particularly on 2 Timothy 3:10-17, I am hoping it will renew our love for the breathed-out word of God. This text reminds me a lot of Proverbs 4:1-2 – it's where the father takes the son aside and gives him sage advice, to help him to keep on the straight and narrow path: 'Listen, my sons, to the instructions of a father; and pay attention so that you may gain understanding. For I give you good teaching; do not abandon my instruction.'

The message in 2 Timothy 3 feels the same. Paul, knowing his end is near and looking to his son in the faith, Timothy, is urging him to keep on in the faith and avoid the dodgy false teaching and stand firm on the inspired word of God. 2 Timothy 3:16 particularly links with the preceding verses and right up to chapter 4:5. Much of what Paul is saying is in preparation for the ministry – preaching as the man of God. But the principles are still transferable to us in general as Christians acting out our faith. I want to think through this text, much like Proverbs 4, as an older Christian speaking parentally into the lives of the young in faith – teaching and training them to grow up into Christian maturity. Eventually becoming women who themselves end up doing the same for others.

So, let's dive in and read the text:

> Now you followed my teaching, conduct, purpose, faith, patience, love, perseverance, persecutions, and sufferings, such as happened to me at Antioch, at Iconium, and at Lystra; what persecutions I endured, and out of them all the Lord rescued me! Indeed, all who want to live in a godly way in Christ Jesus will be persecuted. But evil people and impostors will proceed from bad to worse, deceiving and being deceived. You, however, continue in the things you have learned and become convinced of, knowing from whom you have learned them, and that from childhood you have known the sacred writings which are able to give you the wisdom that leads to salvation through faith which is in Christ Jesus. All Scripture is inspired by God and beneficial for teaching, for rebuke, for correction, for training in righteousness; so that the man or woman of God may be fully capable, equipped for every good work (2 Tim. 3:10–17).

It might be that you're thinking that I'm going to give you some sort of amazing new techniques to help you teach and train your women. If that's your starting point you may be disappointed.[1]

Let me ask you what is it that you want to teach and train your women for? What is your aim and objective? I remember once a guy asked me, 'Why should we train women when they aren't going to teach?' No, I didn't smack him across the back of the head but, reined myself in before answering. It makes me sad to think some people still feel only the 'few' should be taught robustly. So, what is the point? Surely, we want to teach and train so that, as women, they grow in godly maturity, sticking faithfully to the word of God and standing firm to the end. It's not far off the mark from what Paul wants for Timothy.

So, as we look at the text, I'm only going to think briefly about three points that jump out from the text – exemplify godliness (verses 10-11, 13), expect persecution (verse 12), and trust the Word (verse 14-17).

(1) Exemplify godliness (verses 10-11, 13)

Paul is reminding Timothy to think about his example. To remember the way he lived his life, no matter the circumstances.

---

[1] We have a curriculum at Ragged School of Theology that would help you think that through robustly. For more information about taking that elective through distance learning, contact us through our website.

Tony Merida puts it like this, 'Paul's teaching explains his life, and his life explains his teaching.'[2] The life lived out matters.

We can teach so much about who God is, his faithfulness, mercy and love by our godly example. Paul reminds Timothy that he had walked and talked with him along the way. Timothy had seen first-hand how Paul handled the hard times and difficult circumstances. He saw how Paul dealt with people from different cultures and contexts. Timothy saw Paul living out his faith and the apostle taught him much by his actions.

I've used this story loads and it still challenges me. When I was a young Christian 30 years ago, we were being taught about evangelism by a guy called Ian Leitch. I never forgot something he said: 'We might be the only Bible someone reads.' This thought challenges me even today. What does my life, our lives, teach the young Christians around us about God? Just pause and think about that for a second ... What do our lives teach the young Christians around us about God? Our actions matter.

1 Timothy 4:11–12 says, 'Prescribe and teach these things. Let no one look down on your youthfulness,' – this is because Timothy is still young – 'but rather in speech, conduct, love, faith and purity, *show yourself an example of those who believe.*'

Timothy clearly saw Paul's conduct (4:10). He exemplified his purpose in life, his faith, his boundless patience and he showed his compassion, love and perseverance. Timothy saw how Paul handled persecution and suffering – something that's

---

2 David Platt, Daniel L. Akin and Tony Merida, *Christ Centred Exposition: Exalting Jesus in 1 & 2 Timothy & Titus,* B&H Academy, 2013, p. 190.

a given for all Christians. Paul set an example of how to deal well with the trials of life in a godly manner.

Paul wasn't bragging when he said in 1 Corinthians 11:1 'Be imitators of me, just as I also am of Christ.' He fixed his eyes on Christ and exemplified him in all he did. This is what he's saying to Timothy, 'You have seen with your own eyes how I imitated Christ. Now you, son, do likewise.'

In Ephesians 4:1, Paul says, 'Therefore I, the prisoner of the Lord, urge you to walk in a manner worthy of the calling with which you have been called'. He leaves us in little doubt that we are to teach who Christ is through the way we live out our Christian values in the everyday normality of life. So, if we want to teach and train women, we need to set an example of godly maturity in the day to day of life. We need to invite women into our lives, invest in them and show them the real picture, warts and all.

Some of the scariest verses I know are Romans 2:21-23:

> You, therefore, who teach someone else, do you not teach yourself? You who preach that one is not to steal, do you steal? You who say that one is not to commit adultery, do you commit adultery? You who loathe idols, do you rob temples? You who boast in the Law, do you dishonour God?

It freaks me out every time I read these verses because I know there are many times, when I challenge women about something, or when I go through the accountability questions, dwelling on questions I know I'm struggling with myself. I remember last year we were at the staff retreat and, in the middle of a session, Tasha showed me a text from Sol, our music director. She was flying out for the States early the next morning and they needed her to bring additional CDs. The rain was lashing down, it was pitch dark and it was a 2-hour round trip. I remember getting in the car exhausted. I had spent a lot of time travelling, juggling assignments, work and family, not to mention my own sinfulness. As we drove to Edinburgh, I remember being honest with Anna about my struggles and she said to me something like, 'I thought nothing phased you ...' I'm like, 'Are you being serious ...?!' The 2-hour trip turned out to be one of my favourite times as we both took turns each sharing and pointing each other to Christ. We must remember a godly life isn't one that is without trial or struggle – a godly life is one that models Christ and our dependence on him during the trials, standing firm in him.

In her book *Good News for Weary Women*, Elyse Fitzpatrick asks a few poignant questions of women on Facebook and from a focus group. One of the questions is this: 'What are the dumbest things people tell women they have to do in order to be godly?'[3] Here are some of the answers she got:

- Never disagree with other people – especially not your husband
- Only read Christian books (or books with a strong Christian moral)
- Always submit (followed by terrible definition of the word)

---

3 Elyse Fitzpatrick, *Good News for Weary Women*, Tyndale House, 2014, p. 74.

- Never drink beer, wine or any kind of alcohol (even in moderation)
- Don't allow your children to be exposed to certain Disney characters
- Stay with an abusive husband even if you feel threatened (don't even start me on that)
- When your children misbehave, you should be able to quote verses to them (or have them recite verses to you).

When Paul is entreating Timothy to follow his godly example as he emulated Christ, Paul was clear about what kind of attributes we should be displaying as mature, godly Christians: faith, patience, love and perseverance (2 Tim. 3:10).

One guy puts it like this:

> Jesus was the ultimate example of godliness in his incarnation. Jesus was the ultimate picture of humility, integrity, and generosity. His religion was not for show ... He walked by faith ... displayed love like no other. His patience is unparalleled ... He took our judgement and gave us his righteousness. Jesus gave us the greatest example of godliness.[4]

We too must emulate Christ's example. Going back to the Tony Merida quote from earlier about Paul's teaching explaining his life, and his life explaining his teaching ... Can the same be said for us? Does our teaching explain our life and our life explain, illustrate and exemplify what we are teaching? Does what comes out of our mouths truly match how we live?

---

4 Platt et al., *Exalting Jesus in 1 & 2 Timothy & Titus*, p. 193.

(2) Expect persecution (verse 12)

Not only are we to teach by example – we are also to teach the reality of the Christian life. I hate the whole 'Come to Jesus and all your problems will go away.' It's unhelpful, unbiblical, and utter tosh! Not only does Paul remind Timothy of some of the persecutions and sufferings that he had to endure (verse 11) but he is very clear in verse 12 that Christians will be persecuted: 'Indeed, all who desire to live in a godly way in Christ Jesus will be persecuted.' We will suffer for our faith. Philip Towner said this 'Paul does not expand on the purpose of suffering in this letter. Instead, we, along with Timothy, learn simply that it is a normal part of the Christian experience.'[5]

Philippians 1:29 says 'For to you it has been granted for Christ's sake, not only to believe in Him, but also to suffer on His behalf'.

John 15:20 says 'Remember the word that I said to you, "A slave is not greater than his master." If they persecuted Me, they will persecute you as well'.

Basically, Paul and Jesus are both saying that persecution and suffering are an inevitability of the Christian faith. Following Christ comes at a cost. 'Forewarned is forearmed,' as they say. This prior knowledge should give us a tactical advantage, helping us to prepare, to stand firm and be ready to endure what's about to come. We must not only prepare young Christians for what is to come but, also remind them where to run for help when it happens.

---

[5] Philip H. Towner, *1–2 Timothy & Titus: The IVP New Testament Commentary Series,* InterVarsity Press, 1994, p. 198.

> But the Lord stood with me and strengthened me, so that through me the proclamation might be fully accomplished, and that all the Gentiles might hear; and I was rescued out of the lion's mouth. The Lord will rescue me from every evil deed, and will bring me safely to His heavenly kingdom; to Him be the glory forever and ever. Amen (2 Tim. 4:17-18).

Through his glorious resurrection, Christ has triumphed over evil. He is, in fact, seated at the right hand of the Father interceding on our behalf. As Christians we are united with Christ – we aren't alone! He is our rescuer, our strength and our help, no matter what life chucks at us.

One of my favourite verses – in fact if I ever got around to getting a scripture tattooed on myself, it would be this verse – is Song of Solomon 2:16, 'My beloved is mine, and I am his.' It reminds me that as a Christian, I am in Christ, beloved of the creator. That he who spoke the very universe into creation has me tight in his grasp. That one verse reminds me not only who he is, but who I am in him. This helps me keep my eyes fixed on Christ as I keep on keeping on. We need to prepare our girls for the inevitable and remind them who is their source of help: 'God is our refuge and strength, A very ready help in trouble' (Ps. 46:1).

So, as we have thought about teaching and training women, we've considered what our example teaches, we've thought about preparing them for the reality of the walk, and now, lastly, we consider the foundation: the living, breathing, sufficient word of God.

(3) Trust the Word (verses 14-17)

Let's remind ourselves of the text:

> You, however, continue in the things you have learned and become convinced of, knowing from whom you have learned them, and that from childhood you have known the sacred writings which are able to give you the wisdom that leads to salvation through faith which is in Christ Jesus. All Scripture is inspired by God and beneficial for teaching, for rebuke, for correction, for training in righteousness; so that the man or woman of God may be fully capable, equipped for every good work.

We are to build our lives on God's word. As we have been reflecting, we aren't simply to say we believe – and then deny it through the way we live. The Bible not only shapes our beliefs but our lifestyle also. Kent Hughes puts it this way: 'What Christian believe about the Scriptures has everything to do with their countenance and service in faith.'[6] God's word meets our deepest need, transforming us from the inside out.

I want to focus finally on verse 16 for this last section. When Paul speaks of 'All' Scripture when he's speaking to Timothy, he means exactly that: 'All.' Now we could get into the detail about how he gets to the word 'all' including both Old Testament and New Testament, or such as thinking through the reference we see in verses 14–15 as to what he was taught as a child and by whom but this is not the place for detailed analysis. The point I

---

6 Kent R. Hughes and Bryan Chapell, *Preaching the Word: 1–2 Timothy and Titus: To Guard the Deposit*, Crossway, 2012, p. 258.

want to make here is *all* Scripture, the whole Bible, is profitable for teaching, reproof and growing in righteousness. Not just the bits we like, that don't challenge us or aren't difficult to understand.

Kent Hughes shares a story about a preacher called Dr Williams Evans. Evans was preaching one Sunday on the Virgin birth. He opened his Bible and tore out the pages that relate specifically to the birth of Jesus. I suspect there was an audible gasp from the whole congregation at manhandling of the Bible in this way. 'As the tattered scraps floated down towards the congregation, he shouted, "If we can't believe in the virgin birth, let's tear it out of the Bible!"'[7] Then to drive his point home he tore out pages relating to the resurrection, Jesus' miracles, then anything conveying the supernatural. 'The floor was littered with mutilated pages. Finally ... he held up the only remaining portion and said "And this is all we have left – the Sermon on the Mount. And that has no authority for me if a divine Christ didn't preach it."'

This story illustrates the sad situation we find ourselves in many churches who profess Christ. Many don't believe the Word is inspired, or don't believe the miracles happened, or think the birth of Christ is a nice story but just an illustration. And many try to explain away biblical truths because they are unpalatable or make us uncomfortable or are counter-cultural. We hear things like, 'This is not for today' or 'That doesn't matter' because we are not living in biblical times. The word of God is being discarded just as if they were ripping the

---

[7] Hughes and Chapell, *1–2 Timothy and Titus*, p. 257.

very pages out of the Bible. But we, like Timothy in verse 14, must continue in the truth of God's word which we have been convinced of.

Deepak Reju says:

> If you are a Christian who seeks to live faithfully and to live according to God's word, you can help in [al]most every situation. You can't necessarily fix the problem, but you can find ways to help them in their struggle ... A centrepiece of this discipleship culture are the members teaching one another from God's word with the goal of growing in personal holiness. You, as a member, are called to counsel the Word to one another. And whether you realise it or not, you are a soldier who sits on the front lines of the battle in this discipleship culture.[8]

I love this quote from Deepak and use it in my discipleship talk but it sums up practically what Paul is saying: Live faithfully and according to the whole counsel of God's word and teach others to do the same. After all, this Word, is the inspired word of God, breathed out by God himself, for us.

As Peter said: 'But know this first of all, that no prophecy of Scripture becomes a matter of someone's own interpretation, for no prophecy was ever made by an act of human will, but men moved by the Holy Spirit spoke from God' (2 Pet. 1:20–21). The Bible isn't a myth, isn't the stuff of fairy tales, legends or fables. David Helm puts it like this: 'Nothing written down here

---

8 Deepak Reju, *Biblical Counselling Core Seminar: Congregational Counselling Session*, Capitol Hill Baptist Church, 18 December 2011, p. 2.

comes forth from the mind or will of man ... the Scriptures are not a human record of the history of God; rather, they contain the true and authoritative story of God as he enters human history.'[9] The Bible, in its entirety, is the inspired word of God and can be trusted. God's word is profitable for teaching – when we are looking for a book that can help someone with x, y and z, let us remember with the Psalmist to rejoice in this gift that we have in his Word, and remember the great spoils we have – God's word. Psalm 119:162 says, 'I rejoice at Your word, like one who finds great plunder.'

Yes, there are other resources out there and they are great, biblical and helpful – but God's Word is supremely better. Where did Christ go when he was tempted? God's word! We see this in Matthew 4:4, when Jesus answered, 'It is written: "Man shall not live on bread alone, but on every word that comes out of the mouth of God,"' (quoting Deuteronomy 8:3). And again in Matthew 4:10, when he says, '*for it is written:* "You shall worship the Lord your God, and serve him only"' (quoting Deuteronomy 6:13).

'Jesus Christ, God incarnate, leaned on the sufficiency of Scripture in his hour of need.'[10]

I am sure we should follow his example.

---

[9] David R. Helm, *Preaching the Word: 1–2 Peter and Jude: Sharing Christ's Suffering,* Crossway, 2008, p. 219.

[10] Hughes and Chapell, *1–2 Timothy and Titus*, p. 262.

14. Diversity

Andy Constable
Pastor, Niddrie Community Church, Edinburgh

> But now in Christ Jesus you who once were far away have been brought near by the blood of Christ. For he himself is our peace, who has made the two groups one and has destroyed the barrier, the dividing wall of hostility, by setting aside in his flesh the law with its commands and regulations. His purpose was to create in himself one new humanity out of the two, thus making peace, and in one body to reconcile both of them to God through the cross, by which he put to death their hostility. He came and preached peace to you who were far away and peace to those who were near. For through him we both have access to the Father by one Spirit (Eph. 2:13–18).

The Bible teaches us clearly that the gospel breaks down cultural barriers. I am testament to that in Niddrie. I am not from a scheme. I look like I should be a Downton extra, not working with Mez. I was brought up in London in a loving, Christian, middle-class home. My Dad worked in insurance while my mum was a full-time mum. My parents are Christians and they brought me up to know the truths of the gospel.

However, I didn't become a Christian till I was 18. As I grew into my teens, I rejected my parents' faith. I didn't think that Christianity or the church was relevant for my life. I didn't see that I was a sinner and that I needed a Saviour. But God used two events in my teen years to bring me to Christ. The first was a holiday camp where I met a Christian who had been converted from a Muslim home. This shook me up. *Why would a lady leave her faith and family to come to Christ? Why would she leave a comfortable life to be abused physically and mentally by her parents?* Her reason – she had realised that salvation came through Christ alone. It was then that I began to see I needed the forgiveness of Christ.

The second thing happened when I was 18, when I heard a powerful sermon on Isaiah 1 at my home church. I don't know what it was that night, but it felt like every word of that sermon was written for me. The pastor said that we had rebelled against God and that the only way to receive forgiveness for our sins was through putting our faith in Jesus Christ. He also said that we needed not just to believe upon Jesus but also make him Lord of our lives. That night I was heavily convicted. I wasn't a drug taker or a heavy drinker. I've never had a fight with someone physically apart from fisty cuffs with the chaps, but I realised the deep sin in my life. I realised the way that I had rebelled against God. I had tried to do things my own way. I had disrespected my parents. I had been a selfish, self-focused teenager. I realised my pride, lust, anger, jealousy and envy.

Diversity

I was a right sinner. But I also understood that Jesus Christ had forgiven every one of my sins. As the preacher had quoted from Isaiah 1: 'Though your sins are like scarlet, they shall be as white as snow.'

I also realised that if I was going to follow Christ, I needed to do it properly. It was *all* or *nothing*. I knew that I couldn't be like the people of Israel who knew the truth and yet just blatantly disobeyed. I needed to pick up my cross and follow him. One of the first books I read as a Christian was a book called *Don't Waste Your Life*.[1] In it, the author John Piper told me that living for Christ is the best thing in the world and doing anything else is a *waste of time*. He quotes this old hymn which says: 'There's only one life, twill soon be past, only what's done for Christ will last!'[2] This would drive my decisions from then on – and all I wanted to do was tell people about Jesus.

Anyway, fast forward seven years and I've been through uni and I find myself as an intern in Niddrie. I was 25. I was enthusiastic. I wanted to see the world changed by Christ. But I was idealistic and very naive. I didn't have a clue about pastoral work and I didn't have a clue about scheme culture. I mean, I went to a private school in the city of London. I like hummus. I am a cultural outsider if ever there was one. I'm not only a bit posh but I'm also from England – I have a double cultural barrier to get over. I've got no street experience at all. I was one of those guys you duped in town for £30 to get a bag of heroin. I didn't know anything about Valium. I thought everyone was

---

1 John Piper, *Don't Waste Your Life*, IVP, 2005.
2 C. T. Studd (1860–1931), 'Only One Life, Twill Soon Be Past'.

telling the truth, and I thought the guy who was gouching (high on drugs) was just a little bit ill. 'Oh, my, that person is sweating a lot – have they been to the gym?' I was a polite and well-meaning but a pretty clueless intern.

But I've been on staff now for seven years and I understand a little bit more about what is going on. I've made some deep personal friends in Niddrie. I have been involved with discipling men who have come to Christ from Niddrie. I have made many mistakes – many, many! I've been bumped and hurt by relationships – but I understand the dos and don'ts and a bit more of the culture. I realise that not everyone is telling me the truth. I have contextualised my preaching and think I have adapted. It's been a tough seven years but one in which I have grown in my faith and been changed by God. The gospel has broken down culture barriers and allowed me to be used by God in some small way in Niddrie so far.

The questions we are considering here are twofold – first, why have a diverse leadership team? Why have diverse churches? Is this biblical? And, secondly, if we are to be culturally diverse teams, then can middle-class guys and girls make it on a scheme or council estate?

Why have a diverse leadership team?

So, why have a diverse team? Why bother training someone like me to work in a council estate? Why can't the middle-class Christians just stick to their own and their context, and council estate Christians stick to their own? What's the big deal? Three reasons:

Diversity

First, we need culturally diverse teams because Jesus had a culturally diverse team. Jesus chose 12 disciples with very different ways of seeing the world. Yes, they were all Jewish and from Israel, but they were from a whole range of backgrounds. Take Matthew the Tax Collector and Simon the Zealot. They would have been from the opposite ends of the social spectrum. Matthew would have been quite a rich guy. He would have had a fair bit of money. He had a decent job working for the government. He probably would have voted Conservative. Lived in a nice town house. Sent his kids to private rabbi training and most definitely a FIEC conference.

Simon the Zealot on the other hand was a revolutionary. He hated the government and wanted to overthrow it. He probably didn't have a job and would have signed on. He would have lived in a poorer area of Israel. He probably lived in a scheme. And these guys would have been arch enemies because Matthew would have been seen as a traitor. Tax collectors took money off Jews to give to the Roman government. They were greedy as well and often took more than they needed. They were despised by everyone especially the Zealots. These guys would have been like chalk and cheese. These guys would not have got on in normal everyday world. These guys would have hated one another.

And yet Jesus chose these two and put them together in a team. He threw them together and said, 'Get on.' He said more than that – he said that they had to love one another. This must have been difficult. This must have been hard. And yet they both followed Christ. They both were transformed by his grace.

They were both used to bring the gospel to the nations. These weren't the only differences between the disciples. You've also got Peter the big mouth and Thomas who liked to state the facts. James and John were the powerhouse twins. Jesus chose a widely diverse team. They were a useless team to start with. He took some risks. But God used them powerfully to spread the gospel.

Secondly, we need diverse teams because diversity shows the power of the gospel. Jesus says this in John 13:34–35: 'A new command I give you: love one another. As I have loved you, so you must love one another. By this everyone will know that you are my disciples if you love another.' How will people know that we are his disciples? By the way that we love one another. We don't realise sometimes how great a testimony that is. In the everyday world, people stick with their own. People are friends with people who are like them. People stick to their own cultures.

But in the church, everyone is chucked together and forced to get on. In our church, we have people who have been through the social work system and social workers. We have coppers and those who have been in jail. We have former drug addicts and those who have never touched a drug in their life. We have those who have been on the dole all their lives and others who've worked all their lives. *How are all these people supposed to get on?* Well, it's through Jesus. Because at the foot of the cross, there is equal ground as we see that we are *all* sinners and we *all* need Jesus. As that passage in Ephesians says, the dividing wall of hostility has been broken between people groups. Back in the day, it was the Gentiles and Jews – but in our culture in the UK, one divide is middle class and working class. But we are now one big family. And this is a great witness to the world is it not? Where else does this happen?

The problem is that this sounds nice, but unity is easier said than done. It's easier to preach unity in diversity but far harder to put into practice. In the UK, we must confess that as middle-class Christians we can often be quite snobbish. It can come out blatantly. Last year I was at a church and I was speaking to a lady who said that she had been driving through Niddrie. I said, 'Oh yeah? How did you find it?' She said, 'I don't know. I drove as quickly as I could through Niddrie and put my windows up!' There was a perception that Niddrie was this rough place and so I'm not going to stop there. You see, sometimes, we middle-class Christians just see the schemes as rough places where everyone is on drugs and going to take your wallets.

But also, snobbery can come out much more subtly. Middle-class Christians in the past have seen guys from housing schemes come to Christ and what have we done with them? We've used them for testimonies, but we have not trained them for leadership. Middle-class leaders have side-lined housing scheme Christians and just used them as trophies of grace.

Ask yourself this question: how many people are we training in our churches who are *not* tertiary educated people? How many of our leaders come from poorer backgrounds? If your answer is 'none' to both those questions, then there are some major cultural barriers that we have put up that we need to tear down. If that is true of our churches, then there isn't that equality and love that Jesus commanded us. Going back to Jesus' disciples again, both Simon and Matthew were leaders in the church – not just Matthew with his fancy job.

But here is the thing we also need to watch for: snobbery the other way round. A snob is someone who looks down their noses at other people and this happens both ways. The rich look at schemes and think it's full of NEDS and tracksuit-wearing chavs. And the poor look at the rich and think, 'Those people are up themselves. They've had silver spoons in their mouths. I'm not going to work with them. I'm not going to minister with those guys.' But the thing is, to show forth the gospel to the world, we need *both*! Rich and poor. Housing scheme and middle-class, working side by side in the gospel – because it is by our love for one another that we show that we are Jesus' followers.

Let me challenge us all: Jesus took risks with people and used the most unlikely of people to bring the gospel to the nations! That's what God always does. And we need to take risks with people as well. Mez took a risk bringing me on the team with no cultural experience. We took on Natasha, who is a girl who got saved in our scheme, as an intern after she was saved only three months and she is flourishing as a young woman following Christ. And then we have taken risks on others, and they've completely bombed. But the Bible says that risk is right. We step out in faith and trust the Lord for the rest. Don't be all conservative – push doors open and take risks for the glory of Christ.

Diversity

Thirdly, we need culturally diverse teams because every culture has its blind spots. There is good and bad in scheme culture and there is good and bad in middle-class culture. But being in a team of diverse people chisels off the ungodly bits of our culture and helps us to reflect Christ better. When you are just in your own culture, you don't see the blind spots. It's like sin – we are blind to our own blindness. We just think our way is right and that's it.

But when you are forced to question your culture and the way you do things, you grow. Middle-class culture is so individualistic, isn't it? We live in our big houses, going to work each day, without talking to anyone but our family. If you want to meet with someone, it must be put in our diaries. If it's not, then people don't get a look in. One of the great things about being in a scheme is the community. People look after one another. There is always someone to talk to. It's not perfect but there is that closeness. People are flexible and will drop things to help you out. You ask someone how they are, and they tell you their life story. There is an honesty.

But scheme culture is not perfect. Scheme culture can often be very gladiatorial. It can be right in your face and harsh and full of pride. And sometimes it's good having someone who is a bit polite and posh around who is not so argumentative and brings a calmness to things. Housing scheme culture can sometimes be guilty of oversharing. When you ask our guys how they are doing, they tell you how they are doing and tell you about their whole lives. But we must tell our guys sometimes to not share their whole life story with every single person because often it can turn into a pity party. We must be selective with who we talk to. I know these are generalisations, but you get the point. We can learn from one another.

We as a team in Niddrie have all sorts. We have middle-class men and women, we have housing scheme men and women, we have a short beanie-wearer from Ireland, and we have a posh guy from London. All different personalities and temperaments and ways of seeing the world. But we learn from one another and balance each other out. And this is great for our sanctification. We frustrate each other all the time. And this is painful – but it's also great, because our heart issues come out and we are forced to look at ourselves and change. This is a good thing. I always say this: 'The people who annoy us the most God will use to change us the most!'

Can middle-class guys and girls make it on a scheme or council estate?

So, can a middle-class guy make it on a scheme? Can they actually make an impact? I know there are many that are thinking this question as they consider what to do. The lie in recent years is that you need to have the gangster testimony to make it on a scheme. You need to have grown up in a scheme to minister in a scheme. But it's not true – people have been sharing the gospel cross-culturally since Jesus sent out his first disciples. The gospel overcomes barriers and is the power of salvation for everyone who believes, whatever their background. You don't have to be from a scheme to share the gospel with someone from a scheme. You just have to be a willing servant of Jesus Christ.

However, let me also say that it's much easier for someone from a housing scheme to reach out to someone from a housing scheme. There is that shared culture and language there. We have Mez's testimony in book form and hundreds have read it and been touched by it here in Niddrie. But I don't think my testimony of being saved from a roller blade gang would have the same impact if I tried to give it out. There is a connection that goes deep. The guys who have been converted in Niddrie will have a larger impact then I will have.

But middle-class guys can make it when they are part of a team with guys from housing schemes. When they work together. The problem is that in many churches it's just middle-class guys going in by themselves and trying to do it without cultural insiders. But my experience is that you need team, and you need both outsiders and insiders! And this takes hard work and a lot of grace.

So, what things do you need to know if you are a middle-class person working in a scheme? Six quick things:

One, you need to be teachable if you are a cultural outsider. If you are not teachable then you won't make it in any ministry, let alone a housing scheme. As the middle-class guys, we need to know that this is not our own turf and so we need to adapt. Part of this will be to see the invisible culture differences. Just because we speak the same language and are all part of the United Kingdom, we sometimes forget that there are invisible cultural lines. There are major dos and don'ts in schemes culture. I remember when I first came to Niddrie. I would get alongside people and then I would automatically invite them round for dinner. I would go out and buy all the stuff and cook a nice bit of food and then they wouldn't turn up. I didn't realise that people were suspicious of the invites and didn't really go round people's houses for dinner. People socialise at pubs and at footie and in front of TV but don't sit down for a three-course meal for supper. I was used to a middle-class culture where you have dinner parties and invite people for food. We must adapt. If you were going to a Muslim country to share the gospel, then you would have to learn the language, find out about the culture and change your whole lifestyle. Us middle class guys must do the same when we come to a scheme.

Two, if we are going to reach out to a housing scheme then we need, need, need to live in the housing scheme. You will have *no* to very little impact if you live outside the scheme you are trying to reach. Schemes are tight knit communities, and you need to become part of that.

Three, we middle-class guys need to be patient. It's going to take time to build relationships. You are not just going to walk in here and become people's BFFs after a week. Families have lived alongside one another for generations. And we need to know that it takes time to build up relationships. If you are going to work in a scheme, then you need to commit 10 years minimum. I've been here seven years and just beginning to see some fruit in my relationships.

Four, if you are going to work in a scheme then you need to respect the culture. Too often people come into a scheme because they have come to 'help the poor people'. We come in and we highlight all the bad stuff so that we can write back to our prayer support about the terrible drug addicts that we are trying to help. However, we need to respect the culture we come into. There will be bad things but there will be a lot of good as well because there is something the Bible talks about called *common grace*.

When I came to Niddrie, I probably had that 'helping the poor people' view of schemes. But, over the years, I have come to deeply respect, admire and love the culture. There is such a community feel compared to other bits of Edinburgh. People have your backs. There is a rich music and drama culture. I have great friends here. We need to respect the people we are bringing the gospel to. And we need to remember, remember, remember that people are *not projects*! No one likes to be treated in that way. And the thing is, people can smell when you are trying to patronise them or when you are trying to make them into a project, and you will never have an impact with that kind of attitude. Respect the culture.

Five, if you are going to work in a scheme then be authentic. Don't think you have to become all gangster to make it in a scheme. We had a guy from the States who came over to do his testimony and he wanted to try and relate to people so he gave this big testimony about how, as a teenager, he'd struggled with drugs but now he had come off them. When Mez asked him what drug he had struggled with he said cough mixture. As cultural outsiders we must adapt but we don't have to get tattoos or go on a binge to see how it feels to get alongside people. I'm still my goofy old self and people take it or leave it.

But we must be *real* with people. In middle-class land we are quite stand-offish with people. We don't really let people in. We can be quite cold and professional. However, that won't wash in a housing scheme. We must be real with people. We must invite people into our lives and families and homes. We must throw off this image of the pastor sat in his study preparing two sermons a week and being all professional with set hours and that. We must be flexible and out in the community and invite people into our lives. One of the big things if you are going to make it in a scheme is that you must be able to laugh at yourself! You must be ready to take the mick out of people and get the mick taken out of you. You can't take yourself too seriously. If you don't have a sense of humour, then you will never make it in a scheme! Be personal.

Six, if you are going to work in a scheme then know this: that it can be hard being a culture outsider. It's going to take sweat, blood and tears moving into a scheme. I was more comfortable in London, with my uni friends, having my dinner parties. That's natural.

But in time if you stick at it, what happens is that you begin to feel *uncomfortable* around your old circle because you begin to adapt to the new culture you are in. I couldn't imagine living anywhere else but a scheme. This has taken time and it's been hard, but it's been worth it. We need to remember what Jesus says to his disciples: 'everyone who has left houses or brothers or sisters or father or mother or wife or children or fields for my sake will receive a hundred times as much and will inherit eternal life' (Mt. 19:29).

Conclusion

So, here's the thing: we need to better reflect the diversity of our nation in our churches and so we need to plant churches in council estates – but plant them well, with culturally diverse teams that reflect the diversity of our estates.

So, church planter, get diversity on your core team if you are planting in an estate – not just middle-class guys. If you are an established church, then, church pastors, get diversity on your leadership. Get outsiders and insiders, men and women, and push the gospel forward for the sake of Jesus Christ. Jesus did it. The gospel overcomes barriers and by our love for one another people will know we are his disciples!

And a last plea to my housing scheme brothers and sisters, bear with my middle-class guys. I know they can be a bit geeky, misunderstand things, that they can sometimes be patronising and not get the culture. But if they are willing to be teachable, be patient and teach them how to adapt to a housing scheme. It will be good for their soul and yours. And know that lots of middle-class guys have middle-class friends and family with lots of money and that can be helpful when you are running a church!

Epilogue:
Perseverance when we hit the wall

Andy Constable
Pastor, Niddrie Community Church, Edinburgh

The Christian life is not for the faint-hearted. It's a war. We are attacked on all sides. Our flesh wants to take over. Satan wants to tempt us and destroy our witness. And the world is in complete opposition to us. On top of that, we have 'the wall': the times in our Christian walk and ministry when we want to give up. And so, in this Christian walk we need to endure. We need to remain steadfast. We need to persevere through many dangers, toils, and snares.

But here's the thing: this is something that we struggle with in our generation because we are the ones who constantly want to give up and run away when things get tough. We are the ones who want a comfortable life and so we want to skip the endurance bit because it means pain. We are the ones who, if things are taking time, try to speed the process up. Patience, perseverance and steadfastness are alien to our culture. If we hit a wall, we give up. If things get on top, then we run away. But if we are going to grow in the Christian life, if the Lord is going to use us in ministry, then we need to learn to persevere. And that's what James says. So, let's take a look!

> Count it all joy, my brothers, when you meet trials of various kinds, for you know that the testing of your faith produces steadfastness. And let steadfastness have its full effect, that you may be perfect and complete, lacking in nothing (Jas. 1:2–4).

Count trials as all joy

The first thing James says is mind-blowing. Look at verse 2 again: 'Count it *all* joy, my brothers, when you meet trials of various kinds.' When you suffer, you should count it all joy. This is nuts. Think about that for a minute. When we get told we have cancer. When we have a miscarriage. When someone walks away from the faith. When we lose our jobs. When we get persecuted by our family. When people spread rumours in our community that we are paedophiles. When people steal money from us. When our child wakes us up again and again in the night leaving us exhausted. When we feel like life is on top. When ministry feels overwhelming. When the responsibility of being a Christian is getting too much. When we struggle with depression. When we are tempted to go back to the world. We are to count it *all* joy. Suffering is something we try to avoid, isn't it? But to count it joy ... James can't be real, can he? But that's what he says. That's what the Bible says. What does he mean?

Let me make it clear what James *isn't* saying. James is not saying that you should enjoy the pain you are going through. It's not to hop, skip and high five each other and say, 'Yay! Another trial, Lord!' We are not masochists. But what James is saying is that we should see that the Lord is using the trials of life for a purpose so that we can find joy through them. To 'count' here means to 'consider something'. It's to have a settled conviction that the Lord is in control and that he is using trials for our good and his glory! In our Christian culture today, we get things all wrong. We generally have a settled conviction that if we are suffering then God hates us. That God has got something against us. But the Bible says the opposite. He deeply cares for us in our suffering, and he has a purpose and a plan. And this changes how we see suffering.

It's like a mother waiting to give birth. She can go through the morning sickness, the being bloated, the acid reflux, the fatness because she knows that at the end of it, she will have a baby. Well, we can persevere through trials because we know there is a purpose in the sufferings. We can have joy because we know that God is doing something.

Why should we count trials as a joy?

So, what is this plan? Why should we count trials as a joy? James gives us two reasons.

First, trials test whether we are Christians or not. The testing of our faith shows whether we are genuine or not. We see this in the parable of the sower. Jesus says there are those who come to Christ with great joy, then something difficult happens and then they are off. We don't prove that we are Christians by *saying* that we are Christians, but by our actions. The trials of life put the heat on us and expose our hearts. We see very quickly what we love when the microscope of affliction is on us. We see if someone really loves Jesus or not.

It's the same with friendship. How can you tell if you've got a good friend? It's one born in adversity. Someone who sticks with you in the trials of life and doesn't bolt when things get on top. This is the same with us as Christians – the wall shows who's in and who's out. Who's genuine and who's not. What does Jesus say? 'The one who *endures* to the end will be saved' (Mt. 24:13). It's not the one that runs away. It's the one who perseveres and keeps on going till the end. That might be three steps forward and a few back. That might be messy. But the genuine believers keep on going. They stick in.

And this produces that all important *steadfastness* – that solid base from which to live the Christian life in the heat of battle. But, again, we can only learn to persevere when we persevere. We can only learn to endure when we endure. We can only remain steadfast when we keep walking through the struggles. It's like an athlete – they only finish the race if they keep on running through the obstacles of hills, pain barriers, wind and rain. If they give up when things get tough, then they don't finish the race. Or the boxer. They can only learn how to be a great boxer through experience. The more rounds they do, the more they learn. If the boxer stops at the first fight he won't grow. The boxer and the runner can't learn to persevere unless they go through the pain barriers. This is the same in the Christian life.

Think about the apostle Paul. He had this steel-like backbone. He had this solid foundation which no one could shake. While he was in prison, he said 'to live is Christ and to die is gain!' (Phil. 1:21). How did he get to that point where, at death, he did not flinch one bit? It was through sticking near to Jesus during much suffering. He was beaten, mocked, whipped, made homeless, shipwrecked and rejected by his own people – and he persevered.

And that's why Paul prays again and again in the New Testament for himself and the churches he has planted to remain steadfast under trial. This is where we are different to the New Testament believers. We pray that our circumstances would get easier. We pray that God would remove our latest affliction. We want a comfortable life. As you read through the New Testament, you will notice that Christians hardly ever pray for their circumstances to change but they *always* pray that their hearts would honour the Lord through whatever they are going through. Think about the believers in Acts. They have just been persecuted for the first time. What do they pray? They don't say 'O Lord, stop this persecution!' They say, Sovereign Lord, help us to speak your word with boldness! Help us to courageously preach the gospel!

When Paul is suffering from his thorn in the flesh, he prays three times that God would take it away from him. But then God says 'no' – 'My grace is sufficient for you!' And Paul writes:

'I am content with weakness, insults, hardships, persecutions, and calamities. For when I am weak, then I am strong' (2 Cor. 12:10). When Jesus is in the garden, he says, 'Take this cup from me – but not my will but yours be done'! In other words, the secret of prayer during times of trial is that we pray that *we* would change rather than the circumstances. That he would honour his name through us.

So, if you are struggling today with pressure of life or with the pressure of ministry then pray this: 'Lord, help me to persevere. Help me to endure. Help me to remain patient under trials for your glory!' It's the only way we will learn endurance. We don't realise in the ministry how desperately we need God. We don't realise how dependent we are. So, we need to beg God to give us perseverance.

The second reason James gives for counting trials as joy is that it's through steadfastness under trial that we grow spiritually: 'And let steadfastness have its full effect, that you may be perfect and complete, lacking in nothing' (Jas. 1:4). Remaining steadfast under trial means that we grow in godliness and holiness and wholeness. We will lack in nothing. The trials of life work in lots of different ways to make our characters more like Jesus. They humble us. They force us to rely on Christ. They expose our idols. They get us to rethink through our foundations. They teach us patience. They help us to empathise with others. Here's the thing: don't believe the lie that God is not good when you go through trials. The trials of life are doing something in us. There is some good stuff happening that can't happen anywhere else.

Epilogue

Think about a stone that is tossed around in the seas. It's as it gets battered about in the water, against other rocks, that it becomes smooth. Or think about gold. It's only as it is heated to a very high temperature that it becomes refined. The same is true in the Christian life. It's only as the heat of suffering is turned up that we grow spiritually. It's only as the seas rage and we are battered about a bit that our characters are smoothed out. But we must persevere through them to grow! If we run away from the trials of life, then we will not go anywhere spiritually.

We see it with addicts. It's clinically proven that a drug or alcohol addict who runs away from his problems never matures. It's the same with the middle-class Christian who runs from church to church. Or runs from their problems by having holiday after holiday to escape their problems. We will not grow unless we persevere through trials. It's the trials of life that refine us and mature our character.

The lessons we learn under suffering we cannot learn anywhere else. I prayed to grow in patience a few years ago. And the Lord sent me Isaac. Isla slept through the night after three months. Breeze. We thought we would write the next book on how to be perfect parents like us. And then Isaac came along. Never slept. We tried all the same things and yet nothing. I have learnt more about myself and grown more and seen my sin more through this time. I can empathise with parents whose children don't sleep. I'm more patient than I was. It's still tough being woken up several times in the night but we don't react like we used to. We have grown through the process.

When I think about suffering changing us, I think about Joseph. Remember the story. The golden boy, Jacob's son, who gets sold into slavery by his brothers. Who then works hard and is made manager of Potiphar's house. Who then gets falsely accused and ends up in jail, forgotten. He is faithful to the Lord and yet he gets stitched up. Why? Psalm 105:18–19 tells us: 'His feet were hurt with fetters; his neck was put in a collar of iron; until what he had said came to pass, the word of the Lord *tested him.*' The word of the Lord tested him. God was testing him. He was refining his character.

Remember that although Joseph was a man of integrity in Potiphar's house, he had been a *cocky* and *arrogant* teenager as we see earlier on in Genesis. That's what got him sold into slavery by his brothers in the first place. As well as being jealous of him, they didn't like his attitude. And God wanted to humble him, test him and change him for the future.

What's one of our greatest enemies in the Christian walk? Pride. What are young Christians full of? Pride. They get to know the Bible a bit, read the Bible a few times and they think that they are like Jonathan Edwards. They have big mouths and think they have all the answers. They get puffed up. And so, what does the Lord do in his goodness? He humbles. He chops them down to size!

Same with church leaders! What are church leaders full of? Themselves! Their vision. Their way. They think they are going to smash it for Jesus and show everyone how it's done! And what does the Lord send? Suffering! He wants to humble us so that we are reliant not on ourselves but on Jesus. The testing means we take our eyes off ourselves and on to Jesus. We are self-sufficient and proud monsters but when everything is stripped away, we can only turn to one place for help – Jesus. Trials force us to sink into the loving arms of Jesus even deeper. The trials stir up our sins and lead us to the mercy of Jesus.

If you want to do anything worthwhile for the kingdom it will include persevering through times of great suffering. Think about William Carey. He was a great missionary to India and he was the catalyst for a great missionary movement. But it was very difficult for him. First, no one wanted to back him to go out on mission. The older leaders basically said he shouldn't go. Then when he did end up in India, his son died aged five. His wife went a bit mental. And he didn't see anyone get saved for seven years. Yet he persevered and after seven years, the Lord slowly sent a harvest. Think about William Booth. He went on the streets and preached the gospel and guess what he got for this trouble? The church disowned him, and people beat him up in the street and mocked him. It was years before people got converted and the Salvation Army started.

Even here in Niddrie it took seven or eight years before we saw our first converts. It's only at year 10 that we are beginning to see our first leaders come through. It's been messy along the way. It's been difficult. We've seen men and women profess faith, be baptised and then later removed. We've seen growth and then years of backsliding – and then the Lord miraculously bringing people back. We've had people we've sent from scheme to scheme and it's only years later that they are staying stable.

In other words, there have been many times when we have wanted to give up. I remember when I was just exhausted and a guy we were discipling came back stoned and denied it and I sent him away and I just broke down. I couldn't stop crying. The pressure was too much. The decisions too hard. But we must keep on keeping on knowing that Jesus is building his church and the gates of hell will not prevail!

Here is a question for us all: Do you want to be like Jesus? Do we want to see his glory? Do we actually? Then there is no other way than to persevere through the trials of life. We want it easy, but the Bible says – and listen carefully to this – there are no quick fixes! There are no short cuts. The Bible's road to sanctification is uphill and thorny. The benefits of godliness are hard won. And spiritual progress is very slow and painful! And it's repeat, repeat, repeat.

Conclusion

So, the call to us is *don't give up. Keep on going.* Endure. Persevere. But don't persevere in your own strength because you have none, but *rest all your hope* in the Lord Jesus Christ. We need to anchor our whole weight on Jesus, and he will carry us through. He will hold us fast. And he can do this because he has endured the trials of life, counted them all joy, died on the cross and now is seated at the right hand of God.

Hebrews 12:1–2 says this:

> Therefore, since we are surrounded by so great a cloud of witnesses, let us also lay aside every weight, and sin which

clings so closely, and let us run with endurance the race that is set before us, looking to Jesus, the founder and perfecter of our faith, who for the joy that was set before him endured the cross, despising the shame, and is seated at the right hand of the throne of God.

We need to look to Jesus not our circumstances. We are weak but he is strong. Press into Jesus even more and keep running. Keep battling sin. Keep saying 'no' to the world. Keep listening to the truth, not Satan's lies. But know this: 'My flesh and my heart may fail but God is the strength of my heart and my portion forever!' (Ps. 73:26)

20schemes

What are the schemes?

In most of the UK they are known as council estates, in the US they are regarded as the projects, but in Scotland they are called schemes.

What do we do?

20schemes seeks to bring the light of the gospel into Scotland's schemes through church planting and revitalisation.

While it is easy to fixate on the economic and cultural state of the schemes, we believe that the greatest need of each soul in the scheme is spiritual. Most living in Scotland's schemes are spiritually dead and will never be reached by the church, and therefore will never hear the gospel. While charities meet critical social needs, they can't meet the spiritual need that only the local church can address. We believe that gospel-preaching local churches are the best way to reach the dying souls in the schemes for Christ.

To find out more about the work of 20schemes go to
www.20schemes.com